INSTANT ELOQUENCE

Instant Eloquence

A LAZY MAN'S GUIDE
TO PUBLIC SPEAKING

James C. Humes

1817

HARPER & ROW, PUBLISHERS

NEW YORK, EVANSTON

SAN FRANCISCO

LONDON

To my mother and father,
who taught me to love language
as well as life

FIRST EDITION

Designed by Sidney Feinberg

Library of Congress Cataloging in Publication Data

Humes, James C.
   Instant eloquence.
   1. Public speaking. I. Title.
PN4121.H856   808.5'1   72–9124
ISBN 0–06–011996–9

Contents

v

Acknowledgments

I am particularly indebted to five people in the writing of this book: J. D. Williams, who helped make this book possible; Don Whitehead, who encouraged me; George Thayer, who advised me; Bob Smith, who assisted me, and my wife, Dianne, who listened to me.

I want to add that in my collection of humorous stories I have told the facts the way I have heard them or read them. I cannot, however, prove the authenticity in all of them.

Finally in the matter of quotations. I have, for reason of space, not identified the sources. I can, however, substantiate all of them.

Introduction

I am lazy. I am a procrastinator. When I have a speech to give, I often put off to the last minute what should be an all-week job.

If you also hate the thought of holing yourself up in the library for hours on end, this is the book for you.

I am going to save you the pain and agony of elaborate preparation. My formula lets a speech write itself. It's easy. In fact, it's E.A.S.E.—*Exemplify, Amplify, Specify,* and *Electrify.* I'll show you how to run any subject through that formula to produce an instant speech.

And you are going to learn from this book how to turn on instant entertainment—instant erudition—instant eloquence. I will give you the *Ice-Breaker* to start them laughing, the *Mind-Waker* to convince them, and finally the *Soul-Shaker* to leave them inspired.

In Part II you will see collections of these Ice-Breakers, Mind-Wakers, and Soul-Shakers. To find what will turn your particular audience on—all you have to do is turn to the right page.

And that's not all. A good speech is not just the persuasiveness of your message. It is the total impression the speaker makes upon the audience.

I am going to tell you how to have yourself introduced, how to open your speech, how to end your speech and how to handle any hecklers in between.

Mend your speech a little,
Lest it may mar your fortunes
　　　　　—King Lear

PART I

Giving a Speech

1

Spartans, stoics, heroes, saints and gods use a short and positive speech.

—Ralph Waldo Emerson

Most people love getting invitations to speak. They love it all the way up to the day before they have to give it. Then they react the way Abraham Lincoln described the burden of public office—"I feel sometimes like the man who had been ridden out of town on a rail and said 'If it weren't for the honor of the thing, I'd rather walk.' "

And if it weren't for the honor and public attention, most people would, at the last minute, like to cancel the speech rather than go to the trouble of sitting down and writing it. If that is the way you feel—relax. You don't have to sit down and draft a speech! You may have to jot down some ideas on a piece of paper, but you don't have to write it sentence by sentence, paragraph by paragraph. And, as a matter of fact, you are going to find that you will give a much better speech if you don't try to read or memorize a whole written text. To memorize a speech is impossible for most and risky for all. To read a speech aloud and not sound like it is a trick that only professionals can turn. Franklin D. Roosevelt and Ronald Reagan are two that come to mind. The latter was an actor and the former could have been.

All you need to make a good speech are a few notes, if you follow this rule: know what you are talking about. Remember the remark of Count Mirabeau about Robespierre: "That young man will go far as a speaker; he actually seems to believe in what is saying." Pick a subject you believe in and know. Don't try to use that great speech on free enterprise you heard at the association's convention last week—don't try to put in your own words that good article on the generation gap you read in last month's *Reader's Digest*. Talk about what you do, what you know, or what you have seen. I don't care if the Rotary Club *did* request that you speak on family planning. Tell them politely what subject you prefer.

You will get no credit from the audience for how well you spoke on an unfamiliar subject. They will remember only how well you spoke.

The point, then, is to talk about something you know. It could be your job, your hobby, your particular community activity, or your recent vacation. If you still draw a blank after reviewing all these phases of your life, ask yourself what your "pet theory" is— you know, the sort of thing you passionately lecture your friends on after a few beers or in the family recreation room on a Saturday night.

And by a pet theory I don't mean your favorite obsession—like Mr. Dick's "King Charles's head" in *David Copperfield*. No matter how strongly you feel about permissiveness in education or the situation in Indochina, don't speak about them unless you have credentials in those fields. When I was a freshman in the Pennsylvania legislature, a veteran told me, "Don't ever rise to speak in the caucus if the only thing you have to offer is your own opinion or how your constituency feels. They have their own opinions and their own ideas on what the people back home are thinking. If you want to become a member everyone sits up and listens to, talk to them about something you know and they don't."

If you have a profession, it is easy to find subjects in which you have expertise. The doctor can talk on the risk of barbituate dependency; the lawyer on the need for updating a will. Things may seem a bit harder for the businessman or homemaker. But surely the businessman has some ideas on how to improve downtown shopping, and the homemaker some suggestions on how to make streets safer for children.

The topic should be something you have already talked about countless times in conversation, so that when you speak you do so with authority and confidence.

Exemplify

All right—you know what you are going to talk about. Now the question is how to start. As the Chinese say, "A long journey begins with a single step," but the hardest part of the journey often *is* the first step. The answer to that problem is to tell a story—not a funny one—but a human-interest story about one person or one family. Perhaps you can use a fascinating incident or a hardship case you know about.

The lawyer tells the unhappy story of what happened to a widow when her husband forgot to update the will. The doctor relates how a patient died from a barbituate overdose. The civic leader tells of a fire-burned boy who can now play ball again because of United Fund contributions.

Audiences are more interested in people than programs. They want to hear experiences, not abstractions. So you *exemplify*—that is, you cite a particular case or give an example. This is the first part of the E.A.S.E. formula—*Exemplify, Amplify, Specify, Electrify*—and the most important.

This recalls the old story of a farmer who went to return a mule he had bought from his neighbor. He said, "This mule is no good. I thought you said it would understand commands." "It will," said the neighbor, who took a two-by-four from the ground and whacked it on the animal's nose, then said, "Now tell it what you want it to do." "But," the farmer said, "I thought you said it was trained." "It is," replied the neighbor, "but first you have to get its attention."

And the first thing with the audience is to get their attention. *Exemplify*. Talk to them about that unusual experience, that fantastic case. And don't tell it like the insurance adjuster reporting to his company; tell it the way the defense lawyer would picture it to the jury. Think of all the details that add interest and build sympathy.

R. A. (Rab) Butler, former British Chancellor of the Exchequer, says in his *Memoirs:* "Open your [House of Commons] speech with some titillating case or incident, don't start off by giving your arguments *why* or you will have lost them before you have ever begun."

Amplify

Rab Butler was right. Once you have told the story about the poor old widow, then you can begin the statistics about all the other unfortunate people who may be losing out. In other words, you *amplify*—you enlarge upon that one case and tell about similar problems.

The lawyer talks about all the other people who can be hurt by not having an up-to-date will—the children and the grandchildren. He explains what could happen to a person's house, his car, his share in the company if he dies intestate.

The doctor describes all the different tragedies that can happen from letting drugs lie openly around the house. He mentions the various "danger" drugs and talks about each of them that could poison, blind, or burn a child. He discusses those drugs that experimenting adolescents might try to peddle to friends.

Now what about the United Fund chairman who is preparing that kick-off speech at the pledge dinner? Let's see how his notes are shaping up.

EXEMPLIFY: story about Joe Foster, 12 years,
           dark, good-looking, basketball forward
           mother laundress,
           burning of house,
           injuries, legs, couldn't walk,
           therapy at clinic, supported by United Fund,
           now back playing,
           last week, 30 points

AMPLIFY: not only therapy clinic but also
           day-care center,
           outpatient help,
           glaucoma tests for children,
           marital counseling,
           teen-age recreation centers,

Legal-Aid Society,
USO

By the time the United Fund speaker has the headings *Exemplify* and *Amplify* with notes, he is at least half through. Look at it this way—all there is to a speech is explaining a problem and then offering a solution. When you have *exemplified* a problem by describing what happened to one person and then *amplified* it by telling what could happen in many similar situations, you have most of the speech done.

Specify

Now that you have explained the problem, what solution are you going to *specify?* Arthur Larson, who once was a White House speech writer, tells how President Eisenhower, after reading one of his submitted drafts, would call him to the office and say, "Arthur, what's the QED? What's the purpose of the speech? What are we trying to accomplish?"

Eisenhower was no amateur when it came to speeches. (After all, he once served a stint in the Philippines as Douglas MacArthur's ghost writer.) In his no-nonsense military approach, he believed in getting right down to the essentials. A speech that didn't specify any solution or answer was a waste of the audience's time as well as his own.

What is it you are trying to have done? Is it a bond referendum for a new airport? A bill for no-fault auto insurance? Perhaps the businessman wants to propose a downtown shoppers' mall or the housewife wants to recommend stationing traffic guards at the school sites. The lawyer will, of course, offer guidelines for a new will and the doctor a checklist for dangerous drugs.

And what does our civic leader put down beside *Specify?* It may look like this:

SPECIFY: total goal $500,000
          major needs, etc.
          corporate gifts $40,000
          special gifts $10,000

general campaign $450,000
fair share 1 hr. a week

$10,000 $25.00 etc.

Electrify

Demosthenes—a name that personifies great oratory—was once asked to name the three most important attributes of eloquence. He replied, "Action, action, and action." He may have been wrong about putting pebbles in one's mouth but he was right about making a speech. How successful is a speaker if he does not inspire the audience to do anything?

My mother, who had been a schoolteacher, used to tell me about a little girl who had written an essay on Benjamin Franklin. She wrote: "Benjamin Franklin was born in Boston. He moved to Philadelphia. He married. He then discovered electricity."

Whatever turned Ben Franklin on, it is the speaker's job to turn the audience on—to *electrify* them, to galvanize them into action.

And speaking of Ben Franklin, did you know that John Paul Jones named his ship *Bonhomme Richard* after *Poor Richard's Almanac* because something said by Franklin made Jones get out of his seat? Captain Jones had been petitioning French officers to outfit him with a ship without success. Then he read a saying of Poor Richard—never to put in writing what you can ask for in person. So Jones went to see King Louis and got his frigate.

What are you going to have your audience leave their houses to do? What are you going to ask them to get out of their chairs for?

Is it writing to a legislator? Voting yes on a referendum? A speech that demands action from the audience involves them. It gets them out of their easy chairs. It is the difference between a participatory and a spectator sport—between playing tennis and watching it on television.

The lawyer may want his audience to make an appointment to draw up a will and the doctor may want his listeners to take inventory of the medicine chest. And the civic leader jots down these notes as his final request to the United Fund volunteers:

ELECTRIFY: neighborhood captains
pledge cards
"By next week I want to see that everybody has completed his list of calls."

King James I of England would get angry at his lords of the council, who made lots of long speeches but enacted no laws. Once he asked them, "Well, you have sat but what have you hatched?"

A speaker has to ask the audience to do something. A speech that does not isn't a speech but a one-way discussion. An audience cannot respond to a recitation, but they *can* to a request; it is like the Zen symbol of one hand clapping. Applause can be the assent of the audience to the speaker's call to action.

Sometimes it may seem difficult to think of a message for a speech about your trip to Paris or about your collection of porcelain. Perhaps you can give them the do's and don'ts in travel-planning and antique-buying. Perhaps you can urge them to keep a travel diary or to ransack Aunt Minnie's attic. If you do, you are going to turn your audience from passive listeners to active participants.

And a message just can't be tacked onto the end of a speech. It has to be the conclusion that follows from the speech. After all, a message is just another way of describing how a speaker *specifies* what to do in a situation, then *electrifies* the audience into doing something about it. It is the "solution" part of a speech.

At a luncheon in a London hotel Winston Churchill once told the waiter to return his dessert to the kitchen, saying, "Pray take away this pudding, it has no theme." Churchill meant that the pudding was lumpy and loose. Similarly, a speech must hang together and have consistency. And if you follow the E.A.S.E. recipe of *Exemplify, Amplify, Specify,* and *Electrify,* your speech will be a success.

Let's try out the recipe on the subject "Business—Its Role in the Urban Community." (If there is any such thing as a typical audience, it is a trade association or civic organization filled with corporate executives, merchants, salesmen, and the professional men who service businessmen.) Your notes will shape up like this:

EXEMPLIFY: tell story of factory in ghetto,
high fence, uniformed security guards
inside, plush cafeteria and recreation facilities,
yet president is on board of urban coalition

AMPLIFY: bad activities of business
pollution, discrimination (hiring)
no community involvement
what this means to blacks
what this means to community

SPECIFY: legislation
day-care bill, job-training bill
contributions:
funds for recreation center
service:
managerial training,
accounting, bookkeeping, etc.

ELECTRIFY: write Congressman on day care and job training
solicit funds for swimming pool
volunteer service for managerial training,
bookkeeping, etc.

One page of a few notes and there's your speech. All you have done is put your thoughts down beside each of the four categories and you have written your speech. It's E.A.S.E.-y.

You see, E.A.S.E. can be the marginal headings as you, like Lincoln, jot down notes on the back of an old envelope while riding on the train. Then when you're home taking the nightly bath or shower, talk the speech out from your notes. (Somehow the running water, whether in tub or shower, reduces inhibitions for singing arias or declaiming speeches.) And when you're through, time yourself. Is your speech going to take longer than twenty minutes? Don't forget you will probably spend about five minutes with light opening remarks.

I once heard Dr. James Clelland, a noted Presbyterian minister, counsel young seminarians on the length of a sermon. "If you don't strike oil in twenty minutes," he said, "stop boring." Good advice. It is rarely necessary to speak beyond twenty minutes.

Even senators and cabinet members shouldn't deliver commencement addresses over thirty minutes. Remember—a fifteen- to twenty-minute speech gives ample time for questions from the audience. If you are one of a series of speakers, ten minutes is quite enough.

When Congressman Maury Maverick spoke at a TVA dedication in Tennessee, a local politician who preceded him on the platform saw his chance to give his opinion on all the issues. By the time he was finished, Maverick realized that most of the evening was gone. He said it reminded him of some razorback hogs he once saw in Arkansas.

"Those your hogs?" he asked the owner.

"Yes," drawled the farmer.

"Pretty skinny, aren't they? How long does it take to raise them?"

"Three years."

"Isn't that quite a long time?" Maverick asked.

"Well, what's time to a hog?" replied the farmer.

Even if you are the only speaker in an evening, you don't have to speak for more than twenty minutes. Length is no substitute for substance. As Muriel Humphrey told her husband in 1964, "Hubert, to be eternal, you don't have to be endless."

To think that the audience has assembled just to hear you is as intoxicating as drugs and almost as dangerous. There are a score of reasons why people attend dinners, but rarely is it because they want to hear the speaker. For thousands of organizations across the country a dinner or luncheon is the best method of collecting an audience. The dinner has to have a program. And a program usually means a speaker.

The audience is there because its members might be Rotarians or Republicans, because they might have to catch up on the news from fellow alumni or professional colleagues, or because they might enjoy a night out with the boys, or the wives a holiday from doing the dishes.

They are not there because they consider you a better attraction than Merv Griffin or "Marcus Welby, M.D." Remember you are a guest. Don't test the limits of their hospitality. You don't need all night to get your message across. Stand up, speak up—and sit down.

Ghosting a Speech

2

Short words are best and the old words are best of all.
—Winston Churchill

The most terrifying character in my comic-book days was a monster called "The Heap." From a German baron's airplane crash into a swamp there later emerged a mass of glob. As a cloud of ooze The Heap could choke and smother any life in its path.

Similarly, there is a form of inert prose that threatens to smother the force of a speech and the charisma of the speaker. It is the ghost-written speech. Watch the aggressive corporation president or dynamic young senator as he begins to read the speech prepared for him—suddenly he turns into a clerkish bookkeeper. It is as if strange new words and abstruse clauses rise like a fog from the lectern and swallow the speaker up.

Now if you don't want to strangle your boss's voice, if you are called upon to prepare some remarks for him, there is only one way out. Don't write the speech! That's right. Don't write or type out the speech. Speak it. Dictate it to your secretary or to a tape recorder and have someone else put it on paper. When thoughts go through the hand to paper, the result is an article, not a talk. Eloquence never sounds like an editorial and oratory never reads like an obituary.

So what do you do? You start with the E.A.S.E. formula. You get out your yellow legal tablet—tear out four pages, and label the first *Exemplify,* the second *Amplify,* the third *Specify,* and the fourth *Electrify*—and start jotting down notes, not writing sentences.

Let's say you're the junior associate of a law firm and the senior partner has asked you for a speech on crime prevention that he is going to deliver at an annual dinner of the American Legion.

First, how are you going to *exemplify* the problem of crime? Surely there is some dramatic crime story you can use. After thinking for a while, you finally decide to call your newspaper's police reporter.* You reach him and you get your notes for:

EXEMPLIFY: story of 10-year-old girl, raped and killed.
busy freeway outside D.C. in Md.
girl struggling against captor, yelling for help.
100's of people ride by, they see, don't help.
story so commonplace, not even on 1st page
but on 10th.

All right, now that you have your notes for *exemplifying* the problem, how are you going to *amplify* it? What other crime situations develop because no one cares? You think of the cars that are stripped of their parts in the streets in broad daylight, and of the "moving men" who walk right into a vacant home and take out the family goods while nodding to the neighbors.

You jot all this down and then you make another call to your friend who is on the D.A.'s staff. He tells you about the drivers who invite theft by leaving keys in their cars and about the housewives who invite trouble by allowing a "repairman" into their apartments. You then ask for some statistics. You wait on the line while your friend gets the latest fact sheet prepared by the F.B.I. He reads to you that one out of fifty citizens will be a victim of a crime, and one out of every twenty juveniles will commit a criminal act.

By this time you look down at your notes and this is what you have:

AMPLIFY: not only little girls but older girls are raped
while people pass by.
people don't care, not interested, not involved.
couldn't happen to them.
yet people leave keys in cars
girls walk through streets alone at night.
fake moving van
cars stripped in broad daylight

---

* I actually did call a police reporter. The case is a true one.

men disguised as repairmen
1 out of 50, victims of crime
1 out of 20 juveniles commit crimes

After having outlined the problem, what solution are you going to suggest? What programs are you going to *specify?* Where can you find some answers? You think to yourself that there must be a lot of articles on crime prevention in those American Bar Association journals the senior partner has stacked outside his office. (No matter what line of work your boss is in, he receives some monthly trade association magazine full of all kinds of articles proposing innovations or experimental programs in his professional or industrial field.)

You flip through the A.B.A. magazines and discover in an issue six months old a piece entitled "The War on Crime" by a former assistant attorney-general. You skim through it until you find his recommendations. You jot down the ones you think apt.

SPECIFY: better police recruitment, higher pay, incentives
speedier trials
court backlog, too many people out on bail
gun-control laws
state crime commission
better coordination of local efforts and research

Your preparation is now done except for one thing. How is your boss going to *electrify* that group of Legionnaires? How is he going to "turn them on"—to have them do something about the rising crime rate? Certainly he can tell them not to leave their keys in their cars or not to let their wives open doors to strange men. But how can he get them really involved? Is there any organization they should join or service they could volunteer?

You call the police station. They tell you to call the Chamber of Commerce, which has a program. You telephone and get some examples of citizen activities.

ELECTRIFY: citizens *can* enlist
Kiwanis, anti-delinquency program
police work with children
Michigan town

> retired businessmen work out with probationers
> Aetna Life Insurance
> bond program
> Chambers of Commerce in state
> work groups on crime
> Boy Scouts
> church groups

With this outline done, you are ready to deliver the speech. Buzz the secretary and have her come in with her steno pad, then stand up and deliver the speech. Just talk from your notes. It's not difficult and you're better off than that Member of Parliament of whom Churchill said, "He can best be described as one of those orators who, before they get up, do not know what they are going to say; when they are speaking, do not know what they are saying; and when they have sat down, do not know what they have said."

Now, let's look at the first part of your speech—the *exemplify* part—as your secretary brought it back to you triple-spaced.

Legionnaires and Ladies:

There was a story written recently about the death of a ten-year-old girl who was horribly and brutally violated. The girl, who had been abducted in an automobile, was murdered right on one of our busiest freeways as hundreds of automobiles went speeding by—even though her cries could be heard. No assistance was given and the girl died. It happened because nobody wanted to be involved.

That a vicious and terrible crime like this is not unusual is evidenced by the fact that it was not even printed on the first page but on the tenth page of the paper.

Now, even though you might have sounded all right when you talked from your notes to your secretary, that does not mean that your senior partner is going to sound as well. After all, he won't be talking from a few notes, he will be reading words—words that are not his but yours.

Already, if you are not careful, you can see a cloud start to rise off the paper. I call that cloud P.A.L.L.—the deadly pall that seems to drain the life force out of speeches. And P.A.L.L. stands for Passives, Adjectives, Long words and Long sentences. They are the fatty glob that diffuses a crisp talk into a droning discourse.

First, *passives* rob the sentence of life and action. *Passives* put the people most concerned and most involved out of the way. Reporters, when they can't pin down their sources, say, "It is believed . . ." Bureaucrats, when they want to hedge on their recommendations, say, "There is much to be said for . . ."

I remember the story of a mountain couple in West Virginia who were celebrating their golden wedding anniversary. The celebration proved too much for the aged husband. He died of a heart attack and while relatives and neighbors proceeded to turn the celebration into a wake, the widow, very passive, sat in a corner with her knitting. "Poor soul," one of the guests whispered, "the shock must have addled her head." A niece went over to the widow and suggested quite tactfully that she put the knitting away. "Oh, it's all right," said the old lady, "he warn't no blood kin of mine."

Passives can put the central characters in the background—out of the picture. When a line reads "a girl had been abducted," the audience wants to know who did it. And when another line reads, "her cries could be heard," we want to know who heard them. When we use passives we are describing half the scene—a girl abducted, but no abductor, a girl violated but no violator. So go back over the narrative and turn the passives into actives.

If nouns and verbs are the meat and potatoes of language, adjectives (and adverbs) are the dessert. Too many adjectives overweigh the sentences. They make a speaker sound tedious and pompous.

My mother used to say that when a woman finished dressing for an evening occasion, she should always check to see if she was overdressed and had one too many jewels or accessories. "The last thing to do before you leave the house is to see if you can't take one thing off." So check your adjectives and adverbs and see if you shouldn't remove some of them.

Does the speaker *have* to say that the crime was both "vicious and terrible"? Does he *have* to say the girl was "horribly" as well as "brutally" violated and murdered?

Too many big words as well as too many adjectives caused Disraeli to describe Gladstone as "a rhetorician inebriated by the exuberance of his own verbosity" and made Daniel Webster picture a southern colleague as "a preposterous aggregation of heterogeneous paradoxes and perdurable peremptorences."

Churchill didn't say "blood, perspiration, and tears," he didn't say "give us the implements and we will finish the assignment." He used one-syllable Anglo-Saxon words. Why not write "rape" instead of "violate" and "kidnap" instead of "abduct"? And isn't "help" better than "assistance"?

Mark Twain, in advising a man who wanted to run for Congress, told of a young man who ran for the state legislature. He was so anxious to make a good impression that he started going through the dictionary looking for big words to use. But his speeches then became almost impossible to follow and his campaign was making little progress. One day he was milking a cow and practicing his speech at the same time when the cow, evidently disgusted with his harangue, kicked him in the jaw and made him bite off the end of his tongue.

"Well," said the aspiring candidate, "I guess that put an end to the man's political career." "Oh, no," replied Twain. "After that he could use only words of one syllable and it made his speeches so simple and appealing that he was elected every time."

And your speech will be a success every time if you avoid long words and long sentences. The listener just can't keep pace with a long sentence. When a sentence's subject dallies too long with subordinate clauses before catching up with the verb, the hearer loses interest. Let clauses become complex and sentences will become labyrinths.

There is nothing more elegant than the simplicity of a short declarative sentence. It is the style of the psalmist and should be the style of the speaker.

Remember the words of Lord Nelson: "England expects every man to do his duty." What would have happened to England, asked A. P. Herbert, if Nelson had said: "England anticipates that as regards to the current emergency, personnel will face up to the issues and exercise appropriately the functions allocated to their respective occupation groups"?

Go back over the text—cut down the complex sentences as you cut out the polysyllabic words. Take the advice of Henry David Thoreau—"Simplify, simplify."

Legionnaires and Ladies:

Perhaps you missed reading a news story of a murder in our city. After all, it was just another murder—another crime. It was the rape of a little ten-year-old girl. The killer kidnapped the girl. He took her in his car and raped her.

It happened not in a dark alley but on a highway in broad daylight. As more than 100 cars went by, the girl screamed for help. But the people did not seem to care. They did not want to be involved. Even the newspapers regarded the situation as so commonplace that they filed the story on the tenth page.

When you take the P.A.L.L. out of prose, look what happens. Nouns become alive. Words crisp. Sentences quick.

Does it sound staccato, like a radio melodrama? Good! It's supposed to. Radio script is written for the ear—no complex sentences that drone past the ear's ability to comprehend. And if you can't stop a line with a period, don't use a semicolon but a dash. Semicolons go with editorials and legal briefs. But dashes carry a speech's ideas easily and lightly. And a speech without dashes can fall heavily to the ground before ever reaching the audience's ears.

No one in conversation talks with measured sentences where each subject, after long subordinate clauses, finds the predicate. Neither should a speaker. Dashes break up long sentences and force the speaker to talk and not recite.

At about this point, the speech writer says, "But I am not drafting a speech for Orson Welles. I am drafting it for the senior partner. I'm going to have to write in his style."

Nonsense! Don't try to adapt to his style. Just write the simple conversational English that anyone can easily read.

The one question I am asked again and again by people who learn that I have drafted speeches for various national figures is, "Jamie, isn't the hard thing in speech-writing learning how to write in someone else's style?"

The answer is no. The only hard thing in speech-writing is to express someone else's technical jargon in conversational English.

What the speaker wants is a forceful but simple expression of his ideas. The more conversational the speech is, the less it will sound as if he is reading someone else's words. If he gets that type of speech written for him, the corrections he will make will rarely involve style. Except for an occasional word substitution that he feels more comfortable with, the changes will be that of substance, not style. Any speaker can easily tailor a short, simple sentence style to his own taste. All he has to do is season the text with a few of his pet phrases or favorite analogies and the speech becomes an extension of his personality.

During the war Franklin D. Roosevelt ordered a blackout in some Washington buildings. The message came back to him for his approval in this way: "Illumination must be extinguished when premises are not in use."

Roosevelt thundered, "Dammit—why can't they say 'put out the lights when you leave'?"

So follow the advice of Roosevelt, and your speaker will turn on and light up any audience.

Dropping a Name

3

I am always longing to be with men more excellent than myself.

—Charles Lamb

Some forty years ago, after Wiley Post had completed his noteworthy solo flight around the world, he was invited to be a guest at a large civic banquet. In introducing him, the mayor let out all rhetorical stops:

"Fellow citizens, this is the proudest moment of my life—to introduce perhaps the greatest explorer, finest navigator, the bravest aviator the world has ever known.

"Ladies and Gentlemen, the feats of Columbus, Balboa, and Magellan pale into insignificance beside the accomplishments of our great guest, who is honored by every nation and whose name is on everyone's lips. It is my great privilege to give to you our guest, the great . . .

and then a horrible blank look came across the mayor's face. He stooped down and said in an audible whisper to Post, "What did you say your name was?"—and getting the answer he straightened up and declared, "the great Wiley Post."

Post rose in acknowledgment of the introduction:

"Ladies and Gentlemen, as your distinguished Mayor has indicated, I have traveled widely. I have seen the charm of oriental Tokyo, the mystery of Moscow, the vivacity of Vienna, the lure of Paris and the intrigue of Rome. I have had the privilege of being hosted by the kings and emperors of most of the nations of the world, but I want to tell you that never have I visited such a delightful city with such beautiful parks, and such splendid public buildings and graced by such beautiful women and capable men as this, your own renowned city of . . ."

and then Wiley allowed a blank look to come over his face as he leaned over and said in a stage whisper to the mayor, *"What did you say the name of this burg is?"*

Although Wiley Post got his revenge on that particular introducer, he was expressing the frustration that many speakers feel. Introducers often have the faculty of saying things the wrong way. They either exaggerate the ordinary to the point of embarrassment or recite one's chronology to the point of boredom.

There is no way to ensure the right introduction—except one. Write your own. That's right. Write your own introduction and include it when you send the chairman of the dinner your photograph and resumé. Say something in your enclosing letter like: "Because any recital of my biographical statistics would be dull, I have also enclosed a copy of a short introduction that was made of me recently."

Now write one and make it short. Put down the three or four accomplishments that sum up the best in your life. Then think of an anecdote or a story that epitomizes your best qualities:

Ladies and Gentlemen: An introduction is a prologue not a catalogue. So I won't recite the statistics from his resumé—they cover too many fields—that of law, politics, government and writing.

I could say that he was a public defender, that he was elected to the Pennsylvania legislature as its youngest member and that he has served as a member of the White House staff.

But I'd rather tell you about a time in Philadelphia a few summers ago when most of the nation's largest cities were having riots. As warnings came of a possible outbreak, our speaker helped mobilize a squad of fellow lawyers to be round-the-clock "observers" in the police stations. Both the Mayor and the Governor hailed the stabilizing influence of Humes' crew as a major factor in preventing a riot.

The story points out three qualities of our speaker: he likes people, he likes serving people, and he likes serving people in the front-line of action. And action is another name for the title of his speech tonight—"Crisis in the Streets."

The formula for this sort of brief introduction is simple. Mention the profession or field of work. Summarize three or four major achievements in a brief aside (I could tell you . . .), then tell a personal incident or anecdote that highlights some attractive qualities of personality or character.

Don't have any guilt pangs of modesty. "Modesty will be the ruin of you," says the Roman poet Martial in one of his epigrams. And modesty can ruin your speech before you start. If the audience thinks you are just another name to fill up the space on the evening program, they will tune you out before you stand up.

When Ben Wade, referring to the generalship of some Union troops, told Abraham Lincoln, "Anybody will do," Lincoln replied, "Anybody will do for you, but I must have *somebody.*"

The audience wants a somebody—a somebody with distinction or authority. The greater the speaker, the greater the compliment to the audience. Remember the old line: "Shake the hand that shook the hand of John L. Sullivan."

So when, because of false modesty, you run the risk of a poor introduction, you are not only downgrading yourself but also your audience.

If you can't bring yourself to write your own introduction to include in the letter to the program chairman, at least tell him that you want a brief introduction with emphasis on the following facts of your career. Then when you arrive at the dinner, repeat the request to the man who is introducing you. He will appreciate it and probably ask you at that point to write down some of the things you want mentioned in the introduction.

So you may end up writing some sort of abbreviated introduction anyway and it would have been better if it had been typed out instead of scrawled down on the back of the evening's program.

Actually, an introducer is going to thank you for writing an introduction for him—even if he doesn't adopt it completely. The more clearly worded it is, the more likely he is to use it. After all, it will make him look bright and original.

There are many innovative ways to introduce people. First there is the "great man" approach. For example, in the introduction of a lawyer, refer to some great attorneys in history and the paramount quality that distinguished each. You could discuss Edmund Burke and his thoroughness of preparation, then perhaps Clarence Darrow for his mastery of advocacy, and finally Abraham Lincoln for his gift of conciliation. After you have finished elaborating on each of these, show how the speaker has all three of these qualities.

Or try the "quotation method," choosing some apt statements about lawyers:

> Abraham Lincoln said, "As a peacemaker the lawyer has a superior opportunity to be a good man."

> Justice William Brennan wrote: "More than ever before the lawyer is now the policy maker."

> And Cicero once said, "The house of a great lawyer is assuredly the oracular seat of the whole community."

Then show how the speaker fulfills each of the roles—that of the problem solver, the planner, and the community leader.

If you prefer to strike a lighter note, you may want to start off this way:

> In the history of civilization lawyers have not always been regarded as an unmixed blessing. In the fourteenth century, the British king banned them from Parliament.

> Shakespeare in *Henry VI* had Dick (the butcher) say as he plotted a new government: "The first thing we do, let's kill all the lawyers."

> And Dickens had Bumble say in *David Copperfield:* "The law, sir, is an ass."

> Indeed, the explorer Balboa proposed to King Ferdinand in 1523 that no lawyers be allowed in America. But we feel sure that if Shakespeare, Dickens, and Balboa had known our speaker, they might have written differently.

For a funny opening try the introduction I once used for a lawyer friend of mine, Don Whitehead:

> One evening when Prime Minister David Lloyd George was in his native Wales visiting constituents, he was obliged to stop over-

night in a little town. He could find no hotel, so he knocked at the door of a large brick building. A man came to the door and Lloyd George asked, "Can you put me up for the night?" The custodian shook his head, explaining, "This is an insane asylum." "Well," said the Prime Minister, "I must sleep someplace; can't you take care of me? I am David Lloyd George." Replied the custodian, "I say, my dear fellow, we have five Lloyd Georges here already, but I suppose there is always room for one more."

And I might add there is always room for one more Don Whitehead. . . .

There is no end to the ways of presenting people. I once introduced Bill Green, the Congressman from Philadelphia, by listing the qualities he had in common with some of the other great Greens in American history (Duff Green, a member of President Andrew Jackson's "Kitchen Cabinet," Reverend Beriah Green, the founder of the Anti-Slavery Society, William Green, the president of the A.F.L.).

Another time I introduced a district attorney by listing the groups that hated him. With the comment about Grover Cleveland ("They love him for the enemies he has made"), I talked about the enemies he had made—the racketeers, the dope pushers, the juvenile gang heads.

In writing an introduction—even if it is for yourself—be forceful. Think of the person's best side, whether it be the qualities of his personality or that of his profession, then project them. You want to emphasize, not exaggerate. You want to be brief, not biographical.

Negative Name Dropping

The one advantage in writing your own introduction is that you can drop names with impunity. In other words, someone else can tell all about your awards, your achievements, your associations with the great, but you cannot. Name dropping is taboo in polite society.

I recall some years ago at a Georgetown dinner party a former member of the Truman cabinet was holding forth at length about what he had told Dean Acheson and what he had said to the President. As story piled upon story, a weary listener excused himself and went to the kitchen. Soon he came back with a dust-pan and whisk broom and kneeled down to start some sort of cleaning up. When all eyes turned to this curious operation, the talker stopped and asked the broom-wielder what he was doing. "Continue—never mind me," came back the reply. "I'm just sweeping up the dropped names."

People don't like name dropping, in a speech or at a cocktail party. This poses an anomaly. An audience wants to be impressed by the speaker but its members don't want *him* to try to impress them.

Of course, the ideal way is to have the introduction as well as the advance publicity invest you with the proper authority or ex-pertise. But what if the program chairman failed to send your re-lease out to the papers and failed to brief the man who was to present you? You end up having an introduction that gives you all the uniqueness of every other guy who also has a wife, children, a college degree, and a corporate title.

One answer to this problem is to start off with some negative name dropping.

In other words, begin your opening comments with a story which makes fun of you yet also involves association with the mighty.

For example, George Smathers used to begin his speeches by mentioning what a close friend he was of President Kennedy. He would tell how he urged J.F.K. to run for the vice-presidential nomination in 1956, which he lost—how he advised him because of his religion not to run for the presidential nomination in 1960, which he won—and finally how he counseled him not to debate Nixon in 1960—a contest which he also won.

The effect of such an opening is not so much that Smathers was wrong about his advice but rather that he was right about his as-sociations.

Of course this is a technique we all instinctively use. "I just got an invitation to a White House dinner and my name was mis-spelled." "It rained all the time we were at St. Tropez." Even law's hearsay rule adds its sanction to this principle: self-serving state-ments are rejected while declarations against self-interest are be-lieved.

Watch any of television's talk shows—the starlet tells David

Frost how she forgot her lines the time she acted with Helen Hayes, the new cookbook author tells Barbara Walters how she burned the roast the day Julia Child came to dinner.

Think of your own experiences. Is there any accomplishment that you can turn around against yourself? Is there any "negative name dropping" you can incorporate into your opening remarks?

In my own case, I often make fun of my bulky appearance by beginning my remarks this way:

> The introduction mentioned that I have had some years in the practice of law. That is true, but perhaps the toughest time I ever had choosing the right word came not in drafting a will or contract but in writing presidential messages to Congress. In one year the President sends up various messages proposing certain legislation. I particularly remember one on public mass transit. After I had finished it, I had to meet in the cabinet room with White House staffers, and the top men in the Department of Transportation. They all assembled to go over my draft, word by word, and pick it to pieces.
>
> There was a particular sentence in the draft I liked, "We shall eliminate the mass in mass transit," meaning, of course, the congestion. But many of the people around the cabinet table shook their heads when this sentence was read. One said, "Now what the hell does that mean?" And a senior White House counsel to the President looked up from puffing his pipe and observed, "Taking a look at Humes over there, I'll tell you what that sentence 'eliminating the mass in mass transit' means. It means that if the bill is passed by Congress, Humes would never be allowed to take a bus or subway again.

You see that by telling the story I have mentioned my White House background—my association with the President—in a way that breaks the ice with the audience.

Breaking the Ice

4

Laughter is the sensation of feeling good all over, and showing it principally in one place.

—Josh Billings

When my father became a judge at thirty-eight, my mother was interviewed on a local radio station and asked what she thought her primary task would be as a judge's wife. "To keep him from becoming stuffy," she replied.

Although my father was hardly in danger of such a fate, it is often true that the small-town judge is more self-satisfied than a Supreme Court Justice, and that the local school principal is prouder of himself than the president of a university. Particularly in the echelons of government there tends to be an index of pomposity that varies in an inverse ratio according to rank.

Back in 1929, during the Hoover administration, there was a young assistant who reported some diplomatic problems to his boss, the Undersecretary of State, Joseph Cotton. Cotton heard the details of the problem raised by one of our ambassadors abroad and then gave his instructions: "Tell the ambassador to laugh it off." Some hours later the officer returned and announced gravely: "Mr. Secretary, there is no word in the code book or manual for 'laugh.' "

Some speakers act as if they don't know the word laugh. They give the impression that they take themselves much too seriously. And that really turns an audience off. No title or distinction carries with it the license to strut. Dean Acheson used to quote the Arab proverb: "The Ass that goes to Mecca is still an Ass."

The problem is that too often a speaker sounds pompous when he really is not. There is something about facing an audience that makes words seem stilted, gestures frozen, and one's manner wooden.

Even the most articulate of people can have a problem. As columnist Robert Benchley said, turning down a speaking engagement: "A genius on his ass can be an ass on his feet."

The answer is to break the ice. A humorous story can relax the audience and its laughter can set the speaker at ease: the speaker gains confidence from the reaction. Laughter, much more than the automatic applause that might follow the introduction, is a signal of genuine response. It means the audience likes the speaker and is going to listen to what he has to say.

There is no rule, however, that you *have* to begin a speech with a funny story. If you don't feel comfortable telling a joke, don't try. You can still loosen up the audience without it. Any opening lines that show you have a relaxed opinion about yourself will serve the purpose of breaking the ice. Perhaps it can be in reply to the introduction:

I thank the chairman not for his compliment but for the generosity which motivates him to exaggerate so beautifully.

I have always heard that a flattering introduction is like perfume —all right to smell as long as you don't swallow it.

As Bishop Fulton Sheen said, "To applaud, as you just did, at the beginning of the speech, is an act of faith. If you applaud in the middle of my speech, it is an act of hope. And if you applaud at the end of my speech it is an act of charity."

That expansive recital of my alleged list of accomplishments makes me think of the time Chauncey DePew was introduced and his wife leaned over and sarcastically said in a stage whisper, "Hello, God."

Or as Adlai Stevenson used to say: "It is my job today as speaker to talk. It is your job as the audience to listen. If you get finished before I do, please feel free to get up and leave."

Or better still, think of your own light remark. Poke fun at yourself. I remember an ecologist who alluded to his big family this way:

The chairman mentioned all my endeavors in the environmental field but one—my failure in population control.

If you can show yourself to be warm and good-natured, you don't need to be funny. But if you want to tell a joke, make sure it has a point. Never make the mistake of telling a joke for the sake of telling a joke.

Some years ago when Reed Smoot, a Utah Mormon, was elected to the Senate, there was a fight to deny seating him because his religion advocated polygamy—even though Smoot had only one wife. The vote was won when Senator Boise Penrose of Pennsylvania looked over at some of his philandering colleagues who had been so piously beating their breasts about the sanctity of the home, and said, "As for me, I would rather have seated beside me in this chamber a polygamist who doesn't polyg than a monogamist who doesn't monog."

And an audience would rather have a pointed story that wasn't funny than a funny story that wasn't pointed. In other words, never tell a "mother-in-law" or "salesman" story if it doesn't relate to the occasion of the speech—no matter how funny it is. There is only one thing worse than the pointless "funny" story and that is the same story that turns out also not to be very funny.

Let's see what points an opening humorous story can have. The point can be that the introduction was too generous or that the audience's organization has *always* been warm and friendly. Perhaps the story can touch on the idiosyncrasies of the audience's profession, whether law, medicine, or business. Or if the audience is a group of women or students, you may have an anecdote that emphasizes the special roles they play.

Perhaps you know a good story that can be adapted to the subject of your talk. For example, an anecdote that tells in a funny way how things are in a mess can be a prelude to a speech advocating some improvement or reform:

> There are those who think that the situation today holds out little hope of improvement. Their judgment is not unlike that made by a British admiral years ago of an Anglican bishop. The two had gone to school at Eton before World War I. Both were brilliant students, bitter in their rivalry; both went on to great success. One became distinguished as an admiral in the Royal Navy; the other a ranking bishop of the Church of England. Though many years passed, their hate for each other remained undiminished. Years later they en-

countered each other in London's Liverpool Street station. The bishop went over to the admiral in his dark blue uniform and all his braid, and said haughtily, "I say, Conductor, which is the next train to Manchester?"

The admiral, looking at the portly bishop in his belted cassock gown, replied, "Madam, in your condition, I shouldn't think you would be going anywhere."

And, gentlemen, with the condition we find ourselves in today, we might wonder where *we* are going. . . .

In Part II of this book there is a collection of Ice-Breakers that are guaranteed to loosen up the audience at the beginning of any conceivable speech. As speech writer Ted Sorensen once said, quoting John Kennedy, the beginning is the only occasion for a humorous story in a serious speech.

The best stories, however, are the ones you have heard told and you have told yourself with accompanying laughter. Try and see if there is any way you can adapt the punch line. How can you use it to relate to the introduction, to the membership of the audience, or to the message of the speech?

For example, I collect stories about Winston Churchill, whom I often imitate. One of my favorites is that about the run-in with Bessie Braddock:

It was in 1959, when Churchill was at the sunset of his life. He was accustomed to spending most of his time in the antechambers where they dispensed liquid refreshments. On one occasion, the bell rang for a division vote, and Churchill, thoroughly fortified, began wobbling toward the door as the 250-pound Laborite from Liverpool, Bessie Braddock, came waddling toward the same door. There was the inevitable collision, and down went Bessie for the count.

Furious, Bessie got herself off the floor and said, "Sir Winston, you are drunk. Furthermore, you are disgustingly drunk."

Churchill looked at the obese Bessie and replied, "Mrs. Braddock, you are ugly. Furthermore, you are disgustingly ugly. What's more tomorrow I, Winston Churchill, shall be sober."

Now that is a great story but how can I utilize it as an Ice-Breaker with a point? I have been able to use it two ways, the first as a joke for youth:

Today you are students, but tomorrow you are going to be the leaders who are shaping our society.

Or I use it to show that conditions will be changing:

> Up to now much of the business community might have been insensitive to environmental needs but in the future . . .

In another favorite of mine I have adapted the punch line:

> In the Revolutionary War the British House of Commons had at least one conspicuous partisan of the American cause. He was the notorious John Wilkes, whose penchant for taking what in England was the opposite view was only exceeded by his passion for the opposite sex. At one point when he openly hailed an American victory, Lord Sandwich of the King's party attacked his treasonable conduct, saying: "The honorable gentleman from Middlesex will have a limited career in this chamber, for it shall either end on the gallows or by a loathsome disease."
>
> To which Wilkes replied: "The Honorable Lord may well be correct. *It all depends on whether I embrace his programs or embrace his mistress.*"

Now by changing the word "principles" to "programs," I have not really tampered with history, and I have a belly-laugh story with which to introduce any idea or program. ("Now, although I don't have a mistress for you to embrace, I do offer a program . . .")

Another laugh-getter is the anecdote about George Smathers's campaign speech against Claude Pepper. Here I have added a sentence to make it serve as an Ice-Breaker relating to the warmth of the host organization:

> Back in the 1950 senatorial primary campaign in Florida, veteran Claude Pepper was opposed by George Smathers. Pepper was especially strong in the "Bible belt," or northern, section of Florida. To shake the hold Pepper had on these people, Smathers developed a special speech making use of the facts that Pepper, a Harvard Law School graduate, had a niece who was a staff member of a Senate Subcommittee, and a sister who acted in New York.
>
> For the county courthouse rallies, Smathers would say, "Are you aware, my friends, that in his youth Claude Pepper was found— matriculating—in Harvard; that before marriage he habitually indulged in—celibacy. Not only that, he has practiced—nepotism—in Washington with his own niece; and he has a sister who is a—thespian—in wicked Greenwich Village in New York. Worst of all, my Claude Pepper is known all over Washington for his latent tendency toward overt extraversion."

The last sentence does not change the color of the story and it allows the teller to tell or relate it to the audience: "Well, I don't know about Claude Pepper, Ladies and Gentlemen, but after watching the activities of this convention there is nothing latent about your extraversion."

Now stories such as these which are basically true are the best Ice-Breakers. Why? Because the truth is the parachute against falling flat on your face. Even if the audience doesn't break out in laughter, they always enjoy hearing historical gossip.

That's why the historical anecdote is usually better than the latest joke. A joke starts out with an implausible ring to it. And if people don't think it is true, they don't find it as funny.

Creative Communication

Some years ago there was a rumor-spreading group in a national convention. Creative Communication Section was the title. If the group wanted to circulate a story that a certain governor was going to back their presidential candidate, they would invent a situation such as a secret luncheon between the two figures. Delegates who believed the meeting took place would then think an endorsement imminent. The formula for making such a meeting believable was to have the teller be "personal," "particular," and "plausible." In other words, he had to talk as if he had been eyewitness to the scene—as if he were telling it out of his own personal knowledge. Next, he had to be particular in details ("the Governor sent back his martini because there was a lemon twist instead of an olive"). Finally, the story had to be plausible—that is, it was a likely situation that could have happened.

Whatever the ethics of such a campaign strategy, it is good joke-telling advice. Don't begin a joke by saying, "There was this guy in this hotel" or "There was this housewife doing the laundry." You have already blunted the edge of the story by telling them, in effect, it never really happened. People laugh more if they really think the incident did happen to you or to a friend of yours.

A good story for praising the merits of the host organization is one about the meter-man and the surprised housewife. But tell the story as if you knew the unfortunate woman:

I always have had high respect for the Rotary Club and the work that it does in the community. I might say in admiration what a gas-meter man in my town said not long ago under different circumstances.

A most attractive neighbor of mine decided to begin her household chores just after she had gotten her husband off to work. Still dressed in her housecoat, she spied above the washing machine in the basement a big spider in a cobweb. Afraid of getting the web in her hair, which she had just had done the day before, she grabbed the nearest means of protection—her son's football helmet—and, with a baseball bat, she slew the beast. Needing something to wrap up the remains, she took off her housecoat, scooped up the web, and popped it in one motion into the washing machine. At that moment, the meter-man appeared, looked at the woman in her altogether with the baseball bat and football helmet, and said, *"Lady, I don't know what sport you're trying to play, but whatever it is I'm sure rooting for your team."*

And that's how I feel about Rotary, I'm sure rooting for the success of Rotary and the many causes it is supporting.

The story is funny. But it is funnier when the audience thinks it really happened. By the punch line the audience really does believe it happened. They believe so because the teller says it happened to a friend of his and because he describes in so much detail how the incident occurred.

Don't worry about misrepresentation—storytellers have the same sort of license poets do. Even when the audience later realizes that it probably wasn't true, they forgive you because they got so much enjoyment from it.

One good story to tell—as if it actually happened—is this one. I use it when I have been asked to give a speech on a certain topic by an organization, but I want instead to talk about a subject I am more familiar with. For example, my brother, Graham, who is an investment banker, once opened his speech to a group of accountants this way:

When I accepted the invitation to speak tonight your chairman suggested to me that I speak on the accounting revolution. But I remembered the advice a college football player once gave to me—to pick only a subject you know about. Back in my undergraduate days, I had signed up for what was known as the easiest course in college: "New Testament Survey"—taught by a retired minister. The old professor used to give the same examination question every year—"Describe and trace the travels of the Apostle Paul."

Naturally everybody committed to memory a detailed answer to that question. Unfortunately, the year I took it, the professor surprised everyone by handing out a different exam question: "Discuss and criticize the Sermon on the Mount." Everyone immediately got up and walked out except for one football player, "Tiny," who was perhaps the densest student of the class.

When the students came back from vacation, they looked at the posted marks. Everyone failed except Tiny, who got a passing grade. When we asked him what he wrote, he said he started his examination answer with these words: *"Who am I to criticize the words of the master, but I would like to write about the travels of Saint Paul."*

And today I would like to discuss something I know more about and that is the writing of financial statements and annual reports.

Again, note the formula for creative communication—or telling a good story—plausible, personal, and particular. First, the story should be believable. Second, you should tell the story as if it is a part of your own experience. Third, fill the framework for the punch line with the right detail.

Sheridan, the British playwright-politician, once talked about a Parliamentary colleague "who borrowed his jokes and imagined his facts." It is not, however, bad advice for the speaker who wants to tell a good Ice-Breaker.

Collect and file away the good anecdotes you hear—particularly historical ones involving true situations or believable ones that you can tell as happening to you. Then fill in the facts that add thrust to the punch line.

Waking the Mind

5

Those who never quote, in return are seldom quoted.
—Benjamin Disraeli

Cecil B. De Mille was once asked by a fellow movie producer why he had turned out so many films based on the Bible. De Mille answered, "Why let two thousand years of publicity go to waste?"

And why let the wisdom of Plato, the insight of Shakespeare, the wit of Franklin go to waste?

If people love the movies that show what Moses did, they love the speeches that quote what Milton said. You know what sells magazines today—articles featuring VIP's, their likes, their tastes, and their thoughts. And if celebrities can sell articles, they can also sell speeches.

John F. Kennedy was the first of the modern Presidents to make *Bartlett's* a campaign weapon. If Churchill "mobilized the English language and sent it into battle," Kennedy marshaled the quotations of the great and arrayed them as artillery. In one week of campaigning in 1960, Kennedy drew on the wisdom of Robert Frost and Socrates, Dante and Franklin Roosevelt, Charles Dickens and Isaiah.

Kennedy, with the help of his speech writer, Ted Sorensen, had compiled a ready collection of quotations in black notebooks under the headings of such topics as "Government," "Peace," "Youth."

President Nixon, too, has available at the White House his own indexed source of quotations. Where Kennedy would quote the literary as well as the political greats, Nixon prefers to cite the words of statesmen like Edmund Burke, Theodore Roosevelt and, particularly, Woodrow Wilson.

Most of the quotations tapped by Nixon and Kennedy—as well

as many more—are available in the back of my book in the section called Mind-Wakers. Although the section includes the quotations of the great on almost any topic, I suggest that you also start keeping your own.

If you come across some apt remarks as you read *The New York Times* or *Newsweek,* rip them out and file them away. When you have enough of them, sort them out and start your own categories for your own notebook.

The right quotation is like a handsome general—slender and erect with his rank showing. In other words, the cited sentence should be brisk and snappy and the name of the author easily recognizable.

People don't really care what an obscure professor said about ecology and they don't have the time to hear pages of Plato on anything. They want celebrity but also brevity.

Look at these statements on youth:

For God's sake give me the young man who has brains enough to make a fool of himself.—*Robert Louis Stevenson*

For youth, the future is long, the past is short.—*Aristotle*

Almost everything that is great has been done by youth.—*Benjamin Disraeli*

The destiny of any nation depends on the opinions of its young men under twenty-five.—*Goethe*

Certainly the time when the young are to be seen and not heard has gone in America—and gone for good.—*Richard M. Nixon*

Cross-Quotesmanship

Quotations in a speech wake people up. They snap to attention as they hear a great name. Like expert testimony, it helps persuade the unpersuaded and convince the unconvinced.

If your speech is going to advance a certain political proposal, the best way to sell it to your audience is to use the technique of Cross-Quotesmanship.

Cross-Quotesmanship is the citing of "liberals" to prove the merit of "conservative" proposals, and vice-versa. Some classic examples are Franklin D. Roosevelt's one-time assault against "fiscal instability" or Dwight D. Eisenhower's warning on "the military-industrial complex."

When Arthur Schlesinger was attacked as a socialist for supporting the welfare state, he replied by saying his views were those of Winston Churchill and Robert A. Taft.* At the other end of the spectrum, Victor Lasky used anti-Kennedy quotes from the same Arthur Schlesinger as well as from Murray Kempton and Eleanor Roosevelt to puncture the legend of the man in his book *J.F.K.: The Man and the Myth.*

In the Senate, a staff counsel named Bob Smith helped prevent two major pieces of legislation with the use of cross-quotes. To defeat the Direct-Election bill, he made available to the senators opposing it a list of critical statements by such authorities as former Attorney General Nicholas Katzenbach, author Theodore White, and John F. Kennedy.

And in beating down the Equal Rights for Women Amendment, Smith fed to the senators critical remarks from such certified liberals as Cesar Chavez and Margaret Mead. As Bob Smith told his boss Sam Ervin at the time of the fight, "These quotes give us credibility, Senator."

We live today in sort of a McLuhanesque world where the fact of a person saying something is more important than what he says. So when you look through the Mind-Wakers in the back of the book, don't look only for the right quote—look for the right name.

Paragraph Starters

If Mind-Wakers can wake up the audience, they also can wake up the speech writer's mind. How many times has your mind come to a stop at the end of a paragraph?

Mind-Wakers can be paragraph starters. Sometimes a quotation

---

* "The scheme of society for which we stand is the establishment and maintenance of a basic standard of life and labor below which a man or woman, however old or weak, shall not be allowed to fall" (Churchill).

"I believe that the American people feel that production is so great that we can afford to put a floor under the necessities of life" (Taft).

will put the train of thought back on the track. Even if you find that the quotations for your particular subject category are not quite apt, you can always turn to quotations under categories such as Facts and Problem:

Justice Oliver Wendell Holmes once said, "The first step toward improvement is to look the facts in the face."

Shakespeare had the Duke of Vienna say in his play *Measure for Measure,* "All difficulties are easy when they are known."

As Léon Gambetta advised after the German defeat of France in 1871, "Let us study our misfortunes and go back to the causes."

And Mind-Wakers can start speeches as well as paragraphs. Almost any speech can begin with quotations about history:

In front of the Archives Building in Washington there is a statue inscribed with the phrase from Shakespeare's *Tempest:* What is past is prologue.

The Patrick Henry who pleaded for "liberty or death" also warned: "I know of no way of judging the future save by the past."

As the Danish philosopher Søren Kierkegaard told us, "Life must be lived forwards but can only be understood backwards."

One passage that perhaps has started the most speeches is the sentence that opens Dickens's *A Tale of Two Cities*—even John Kennedy once started a speech by saying, "It was the best of times, it was the worst of times."

On the other hand, Richard Nixon often begins remarks with an explanation of the word "crisis" in Chinese—telling how it is made by joining two picture characters, one meaning "danger," the other "opportunity."

At any rate, either of these Mind-Wakers can launch a speaker into his address:

It is "the worst of times" because of the danger of pollution, but it can be "the best of times" because we have the technology to solve it. . . .

Nixon can talk about the "crisis" in the Mideast—with the danger of war imminent and yet the opportunity for America to help negotiate a peace.

Word-Stories

Like the Chinese word for crisis, Mind-Wakers can also be Word-Stories—an interesting as well as arresting way to capture the audience's attention:

Did you know that the Chinese invented the idea of a "credibility gap" in government? Their word for a public official is a picture showing two mouths under one roof.

From the Japanese we learn that the word *wari-kiru* means cutting through a problem to find the core, and the word *tenko* describes the behavior of one who does not live up to his principles.

The Hawaiians have no word for *weather* because the climate is so good, but the Eskimos have no word for *thank you* because helping a fellow man is a duty where the climate is so stark.

Tell them the story of Baliol, King of Scotland, who was called "Toom Tabard" or "The Empty Cloak" because he had no guts, or bring into your speech the fact that the nickname of the English King Ethelred was not really "The Unready" but "the Redeless" because he never listened.

Take the audience's mind back to the Holy Land to the Sermon on the Mount, and explain that the dictum "Blessed are the Meek,"* did *not* mean to be passive, but to prepare oneself and accept training. Or let them sit in the legislature of Athens where our word *problem* then meant a bill that had to be passed immediately.

Contemporary Antiquities

Even better than taking the audience back to the problems of the world is to let the sages of that world talk about *our* problems. There is nothing quite like hearing the Romans complain of traffic congestion with chariots or finding that the Chinese had inflation two thousand years ago so severe that they had to use wheelbarrows to carry their money. Such "contemporary antiquities" are

---

* The Greek word *praos* has been mistakenly translated as meek; it means ready to accept discipline; to be trainable, educable.

real show-stoppers. People love to hear Demosthenes denounce demagogic politicians, Cato complain about the young, and Shakespeare condemn pollution.

Misery loves company—and that company can be yesteryear's prophet as well as today's neighbor. Not long ago Richard Nixon told an audience about a writer who said, "Many thinking people believe America has seen its best days," and then added that the author was a Revolutionary patriot, James Allen, who jotted that entry in his diary in July 1775.

Another contemporary antiquity that is currently traveling the speech circuits begins:

> The earth is degenerating these days. Bribery and corruption abound. Children no longer mind parents. Every man wants to write a book and it is evident that the end of the world is approaching fast.

And so words on an Assyrian tablet of five thousand years ago reads like the morning paper.

Alice in Wonderland

Rather than antique lands, a few speakers prefer the "never-never." Some college professors will cite Lewis Carroll as an authority the way country preachers do the Bible.

If the topic is the environment, they will say that the problem is "much of a muchness" (The Mad Hatter) and that "It takes all the running you can do to keep in the same place" (The Queen to Alice, *Through the Looking-Glass*).

When they talk about pollution waste, they will quote the exchange between the Walrus and the Carpenter:

> "If seven maids with seven mops
> Swept it for half a year,
> Do you suppose," the Walrus said,
> "That they could get it clear?"
> "I doubt it," said the Carpenter,
> And shed a bitter tear.

Or, in the matter of the population explosion, they will repeat Alice's answer to the White Queen:

The White Queen asks: "What's one and one and one and one and one and one and one and one and one and one?" And Alice replies: "I don't know. I lost count."

And in painting future consequences they will cite the same White Queen: "It's a poor memory that only works backwards."

Finally, in the matter of what should be done, there is the exchange between the Cheshire Cat and Alice.

She asks: "Would you tell me, please, which way I ought to go from here?"

"That depends a good deal on where you want to get to," said the cat.

You may think that quoting Alice is a bit precious for some audiences—but never be too sure. Whether it's *Wonderland*'s Lewis Carroll or Maryland's Charles Carroll, people love the quotations of the famous—be they writers of Jabberwocky or signers of the Declaration. Remember what the cabdriver said to Adlai Stevenson in 1952 when the Democratic presidential candidate asked him whether he thought his speeches were going over the head of the average man. The cabdriver pondered the question. Then replied, "Well, Governor, I understand you, but I'm not so sure about the average man."

Shaking the Soul

6

The finest eloquence is that which gets things done.
—David Lloyd George

Ted Sorensen, in his biography, *Kennedy,* writes how in the 1960 presidential campaign he would flash reminders for "appropriate speech endings" for John Kennedy with the phrases "General Marshall," "Rising Sun," or "Candles." The "Marshall" one meant that Kennedy would end his speech by saying:

> During the Korean War, a young American was called out of the ranks by the Chinese Captain who said to him, "What do you think of General George C. Marshall?" He replied, "I think George Marshall is a great American." He was hit by the butt of a rifle and knocked to the ground.
>
> They picked him up and said, "What do you think of George Marshall now?" He said, "I think George Marshall is a great American."
>
> This time there was no rifle butt because they had classified him and determined upon his courage.
>
> I think, as individuals and as Americans, we too, are going to be called to give an affirmative answer. . . .

"Rising Sun" indicated this story:

> At the close of the Constitutional Convention, Benjamin Franklin rose and made an observation about the chair from which General Washington had been presiding.
>
> On the chair was the design of a sun low on the horizon, and many of the delegates had wondered whether it was a rising or a setting sun.
>
> "We know now," Franklin said. "It is a rising sun and the beginning of a great new day!"

And the "Candles" prompted this closing:

> In 1780 in Hartford, Connecticut, the skies at noon turned one day from blue to gray and by midafternoon the city had darkened over so densely that, in that religious age, men fell on their knees and begged a final blessing before the end came. The Connecticut House of Representatives was in session and many of the members clamored for immediate adjournment. The Speaker of the House, one Colonel Davenport, came to his feet and he silenced the din with these words: "The day of judgment is either approaching or it is not. If it is not, there is no cause for adjournment. If it is, I choose to be found doing my duty. I move, therefore, that candles be brought to enlighten this hall of democracy."
> Let each of us in this difficult and somber time in our history bring and light candles to help illuminate our country's way.

The Davenport story is the perfect Soul-Shaker—that is, an inspirational vignette out of history to lift the audience right out of their seats. It strikes at the soul's deepest chords—Founding Fathers, God, duty. . . .

Imagine yourself describing the total blackness of that June summer day. As you tell how the noise of the anxious assembly died down when Colonel Davenport rose to speak, you'll hear your own audience become quiet. Then in a hushed voice you ask them to light their own candles against the darkness.

I guarantee you that no matter how inadequate the speech before, you will have left the audience inspired to do something.

Ninety per cent of a speech's impression can be how you end your talk. The Soul-Shaker can be the electrifier—the thing that turns the audience on, the trigger that motivates the audience to act—to vote, to pass a resolution, to write their Congressman, to pledge their contribution.

In Shakespeare's *Henry IV,* Glendower says, "I can call spirits from the vasty deep."

And Hotspur replies, "Why so can I: or so can any man. But will they come when you do call for them?"

A good Soul-Shaker will make the audience respond. It will make them want to take immediate action. Think how General MacArthur closed his address to Congress by quoting the words of the old barracks refrain, "Old soldiers never die . . ." or remember how Winston Churchill ended a speech in World War II with a line by Arthur Clough: "But westward, look, the land is bright. . . ."*

In the back of the book there are scores of Soul-Shakers for use to all audiences, but you would do best to develop your own —some from your own experience—what your father said when you went off to college—what a soldier wrote you from Vietnam. Think of situations that build anticipation such as a response to a question.

> As a boy, I asked my grandfather once what was his greatest satisfaction in life and he replied . . .

> On my first day in the first job I ever had, I asked my boss what was my responsibility and he said, "Son . . ."

Some of the best Soul-Shakers are framed as answers to questions:

> When Thucydides was asked when justice would come to Athens, the philosopher replied, "Justice will not come to Athens until those who are not injured are as indignant as those who are injured."

> When Dr. William Menninger of the Mayo Clinic was asked how to achieve mental health, he replied, "Find a mission in life and take it seriously."

Think about the audience you are going to face. Who are some of the heroes of that organization? Was the founder of national stature? If so, the local library must have a book on him. Read or at least skim through it. Find a statement of the man as he mounted a dramatic moment.

I remember once preparing a speech to be given to the Justinian Society (an organization made up of lawyers of Italian ancestry). I got out a book on Justinian and searched out a statement contingent on his ordering the codifying of all the laws and the statutes.

---

* . . . And not by eastern windows only
 When daylight comes, comes in the light
 In the front the sun climbs slow, how slowly,
 But westward, look, the land is bright.

The audience, which had only the vaguest conception of who Justinian really was, was thrilled by the closing. And they were touched by the fact that I had studied him and knew something about him.

How many people *really* know something about the man who founded their town, or the man for whom their town was named? Most likely he played some role in the development of America—the War for Independence, the Civil War—even the act of opening a new territory or founding a new settlement touches on the Soul-Shaker themes of vision or opportunity.

I recall a Soul-Shaker I wrote for a hospital fund-raising cause in Allentown.

> Some 230 years ago there was a campaign to build a State House, a home for the Provincial Assembly of Pennsylvania. When the project aborted for lack of funds, one lawyer who believed in the future of Pennsylvania came forward. His name was William Allen. He was the financier of what we now know as Independence Hall and later the founder of what we know as Allentown.

Hardly anyone in the audience knew about Allen's connection with Independence Hall. All I had done was to look up Allentown in the library and I found out that it was named for William Allen, who helped finance the building of Independence Hall.

Look up the town's history. What does the name mean? Did a famous battle take place nearby? What notable person was born there? Who passed through there? Perhaps Benjamin Franklin, George Washington, Abraham Lincoln, or Robert E. Lee. I remember a Soul-Shaker I gave in a town which General Lafayette had once visited in his several tours of America.

> In 1826 General Lafayette made a return visit to the country whose independence he helped secure. Anxious to see how this experiment in self-government was making out, he toured the cities and towns of the emerging republic. Among the towns he visited was this one. And when he finished the trip, he wrote back to a colleague these words which evinced his faith in the American democracy:
> "They are solving the magnificent problem of liberty."

If some statesman has a connection with the city, check his name in *Bartlett's* and see if you can't find a good adaptable quotation for the occasion. Look through the collection of Mind-Wakers in the back of this book. Almost any of them under the sections "Action," "Commitment," "Faith," "Future," "Involvement," "Purpose," "Renewal," "Service," and "Vision" can be used as a Soul-Shaker.

The point is that many of the Mind-Wakers are potential Soul-Shakers. All you have to do is to frame the quotation with dramatic impact. What was the speaker doing at the time? What was the condition of the world?

For example, any quotation by Lincoln evokes a poignant note:

> Let us all bear in mind the words of Abraham Lincoln as he led our forefathers through the turmoil of the Civil War: "Let us have faith that right makes might, and in that faith let us to the end dare to do our duty as we understand it."
>
> Or: "I leave you hoping that the lamp of liberty will burn in your bosoms until there shall no longer be a doubt that all men are created equal."

Richard Nixon is one of those who has used Lincoln quotations "to end on the up-beat," as he says. In acceptance speeches for the Republican nomination both in 1960 and in 1972, he used Lincoln's reply to the Methodist clergy: "It is not a question of whether God is on our side, but whether we are on His side." And in 1968 he closed with Lincoln's farewell words to Springfield.

> Today I leave you. I go to assume a task more difficult than that which devolved upon General Washington. The great God which guided him must help me. Without that assistance I shall surely fail: With it, I cannot fail.

Nixon described such Soul-Shaker stories as "parables." Again and again Jim Keogh and Ray Price would say as they presided over the White House weekly staff meeting of the speech writers: "The one message I have from the President today is 'more parables.' "

Ceremonial Remarks

President Nixon has used "parables" or Soul-Shakers not only as an ending for a major speech but also as a beginning point for some more informal remarks. Actually, most of the speaking assignments for the President are not the ones we see televised, like the State of the Union Address, but the brief comments he makes every day as Chief of State—toasting foreign dignitaries at state dinners, presiding over the lighting of a Christmas tree, or welcoming a 4H Club delegation in the White House Rose Garden.*

The advantage of using Soul-Shakers for such occasions is that the President has a story around which to build his off-the-cuff remarks. He does not have to memorize, line by line, the whole text of remarks prepared for him; he just has to remember the "parable" and then think of two or three points that illustrate the significance of the story.

For example, in toasting the Shah of Iran in 1969, he recalled that Ecbatana, the ancient capital of Persia, meant "meeting place of diverse peoples for peace."

At another state dinner he recounted the letter John Adams wrote to his wife, Abigail, the first night he stayed in the White House:

> Before I end my letter, I pray Heaven to bestow the best of blessings on this house and all that shall hereafter inhabit it. May none but wise and honest men ever rule under this roof.

For the retirement of Chief Justice Earl Warren he used as his jumping-off point what Will Rogers said at the death of Chief Justice William Howard Taft: "It is great to be great but it is greater to be human."

Now if you ever know you are going to be called on to award a watch to the retiring company treasurer or toast the bride at a wedding reception, think of the right Soul-Shaker to set the mood and your few remarks will automatically flow out of the story.

For the retirement of a colleague of the State Department, I once said:

> When Thomas Jefferson arrived in Paris to take the position of Minister to France, he was asked if he came to replace Benjamin Franklin.

---

* Unlike President Johnson, Nixon has not read from a text on such occasions. His usual practice has been to glance at some "suggested remarks" in the privacy of the Oval Office and then go out to the garden to greet guests without any notes.

Jefferson replied, "No one can replace Dr. Franklin. I am only succeeding him."

And no one can replace our good friend . . .

And at a dinner honoring my cousin Ambassador John Humes, I started a toast to his wife, Jean, with this story:

> Some years ago at the Savoy Hotel in London there was a banquet attended by most of the notables of Britain, including the Prime Minister, Sir Winston Churchill, and his wife, Lady Churchill. It was a tradition at this particular banquet to put on some sort of public charade before the main address by the guest speaker. The game that night was: "If you couldn't be who you are, who would you like to be?" Each of the dignitaries at the head table answered the question in their own way but of course the audience was breathless with anticipation as to how Churchill would respond. After all, a Churchill wouldn't want to be a Julius Caesar or Napoleon. When Churchill, as ranking member of the occasion, rose as the last speaker, he said, "If I can't be who I am, I would most like to be"—and then the seventy-eight-year-old Sir Winston turned to touch his wife's hand—"Lady Churchill's second husband."

After a story like that men as well as women will get a little moist-eyed. At a bridal party all you have to do is say a few words on why the groom will someday feel the same way about his bride, and you have your toast.

But sometimes you need more than a few words. You are asked to speak at a dedication of a building, or to give the eulogy at a memorial service. Here more than just a Soul-Shaker and a few sentences are needed. You need to expand your theme.

The E.A.S.E. formula will not work. You are not proposing a reform or solution, you are celebrating a person or an occasion.

As a White House speech writer I often had to prepare such remarks of commemoration or greetings for President Nixon. It is these messages that a Lyndon Johnson speech writer once called "Rose Garden Rubbish."* For such an assignment, I took the advice my fellow White House speech writer Bill Safire once gave me. He said that for the occasion of Nixon's return from Europe in

---

* Peter Benchley, son of the famous writer-humorist, so entitled an article for *Life* describing his trials in ghost writing such toasts and greetings.

1969 he took and adapted a story about Pitt, after he had been hosted by some European delegations:

> Find an anecdote that applies and think of the theme it describes. The theme in this case is "the understanding" gained from the meetings and discussions. First you write how much better America now understands the problems of Europe, then some paragraphs on how the countries better understand some of our problems, and finally how much they now have come to understand better some of their own problems.

I call this formula for ceremonial remarks the *Symphonic Method*. First find the Soul-Shaker that best illustrates the theme you want to stress—such as service. Then think of two or three variations to play upon that theme—how the man honored has served his country—how he has served his community—how he has served his family.

Once when I had to prepare eulogistic remarks at a court memorial service for a judge, I quoted the words from the speech that Horace Mann gave just before his death:

> Be ashamed to die until you have won some victory for humanity.

With that as a starting point I discussed in turn four of the judge's major accomplishments during his life and what each of them meant to the community.

Another time I was asked to speak at the dedication of a boys' school in England which William Penn had once attended.

> In my home city of Philadelphia the highest landmark is the statue of the man who attended this school. As William Penn looks out over the city and Commonwealth that he founded, the biblical words that are inscribed on the base of that statue come quickly to mind:
>
> Lo, I go to prepare a place before thee.
>
> Today the board of governors, the faculty, and the students each have a role in preparing a place here in England, as their fellow townsman William Penn once did in America.

The remarks that followed dwelt on the obligations of each group—the board of governors to the school, the faculty to the students, and the students to succeeding generations of students.

Some speakers under-prepare for the ceremonial occasion because they think it is time for sentiment, not substance. Truly great orators like Douglas MacArthur never make this mistake. MacArthur realized that an audience can be more inspired by the commemoration of a person than by the consideration of a program. The highest eloquence—from Pericles' orations to Lincoln's Gettysburg Address—comes from such occasions.

When I delivered a eulogy for John Kennedy in 1963 in the Pennsylvania House of Representatives, the House parliamentarian, who had served there for over fifty years, told me it was the finest address he had heard in his lifetime.* But in truth it was not the poignancy of my remarks but that of the occasion—the assassination of a young President.

It is the mood of the scene that is moving. The audience wants to let out their feelings. And when they do, they often mistake their reaction to the occasion as their reaction to the speech.

When you tell a Soul-Shaker, you are borrowing the emotional impact of a great occasion. You are staging the drama of a great moment and using it to heighten the feelings of your own audience.

An orator like Churchill recognized this technique and used it. Remember his famous speech in June 1941. He knew how he felt when he received from Roosevelt the Longfellow poem that the President had written in his own hand. So he closed his speech by asking the House of Commons if he could read the verse to them:

> Sail on, O Ship of State!
> Sail on, O Union, strong and great!
> Humanity with all its fears,

---

* I opened my remarks by telling about the inscription at Thermopylae which in fact Kennedy had himself once cited: "There is carved on the rocks of Thermopylae in Greece where a few Greeks in 480 B.C. valiantly withstood thousands of Persians, the inscription testifying to the sacrifice of those who sacrificed their lives in the defense of freedom. The poetic lines read:

> Go, passer-by and to Sparta tell
> That we in faithful service fell.

> With all its hopes of future years,
> Is hanging breathless on thy fate!

Then Churchill looked up from reading the verse and said: "What is the answer that I shall give to this great American leader? Here it is: Give us the tools and we will finish the job."

And at the risk of anticlimax let me add—here are the tools for your speech. Whether you want to finish a speech or begin ceremonial remarks, make use of the Soul-Shakers to make your talk eloquent.

Squelching the Hecklers

7

Wit is cultural insolence.
                    —Aristotle

There is nothing more frustrating than finding the course of your prepared remarks derailed by a heckler. I remember when I was in school in England, trying to deliver an address in debate competition. Being the only American in the school I had worked hard polishing my speech, but when I was a third of the way through it, a boy stood in the back, saying, "I rise on grounds of personal privilege." He kept repeating the sentence louder and louder until I was finally forced to recognize him. Knowing a little about parliamentary rules I said, "You know that parliamentary rules do not allow interruption or the questioning of my argument on grounds of personal privilege. That privilege is only granted for some external emergency like the microphone not working or the lights going out."

My interrupter replied, "The speaker is correct. My request is based on such considerations. I rise to move that the windows be opened. There seems to be too much hot air being emitted in this chamber."

Of course, I was devastated by such sophisticated heckling and lost the debate. In retrospect I might have turned down the request by saying "Knowing that matter travels faster in heat it was my hope that the higher velocity of my words could better penetrate the density of your skull."

That is what the French author Denis Diderot called "staircase wit"—that is, thinking of the retort later when going up to bed.

But few of us have the presence of mind to think of the apt rejoinder at the time. We envy the ready wit of people like William

Howard Taft who, when a hurled cabbage landed at his feet, leaned over to pick it up and said, "I see a member of the audience has lost his head."

Most speakers have neither the innate talent for the repartee of Churchill, Disraeli, or Sheridan nor the daily give-and-take experience of a forum like the House of Commons to hone what talents they have.

Even Winston Churchill, the most quoted master of repartee, used to develop most of his bons mots beforehand. His namesake, Winston Churchill II, once told me that his grandfather used to wait days or even months for the right moment to shoot back his ready rejoinder.

Just getting yourself emotionally prepared for the possibility of a heckler is half the battle. Think what you are going to reply if a heckler yells, "How many babies did you kill today?" The one thing never to do is to give a rational answer. I pity the poor speaker who says "The Vietcong kill more babies," or "We aren't killing babies now."

If you begin an impassioned defense of American foreign policy, you have already lost. You are on the defensive, playing his game by his rules. The best way is to start your own game, making him play your way.

Over the last few years I have addressed many college audiences on foreign policy. Not unexpectedly, there have been a few hecklers. When one began yelling something like "warmonger," I would ask him, "What's your birthday?" Usually there is a hesitant answer like "January second." Then with a shrug to the audience I say, "I thought so. A Capricorn—you know, the goat—always trying to butt in." Now since most of the college crowd today follow astrology, this never fails to bring a laugh at the expense of the heckler. You have made him play your game and you've won. With the game over, you can return to your speech.

If you like this routine, you can use it to fit just about all the Zodiac signs:

Sagittarius (November 23–December 21)—"Wouldn't you know it? He's only half human—the other half is a horse's ass."

Scorpio (October 24–November 22)—"Of course, the scorpion. But once they sting, they drop dead."

Libra (September 24–October 23)—"A Libra, a person with the scales—people always trying to 'weigh' in."

Virgo (August 24–September 23)—"Ah, the perennial virgin—incapable of having anything penetrate—a speech or anything else."

Leo (July 24–August 23)—"Of course—the big showoff always trying to get the lion's share of attention."

Cancer (June 22–July 23)—"Wouldn't you know it. There's a crab in every audience."

Gemini (May 22–June 21)—"Ah, the perfect 'schizo'—never know whether they're coming or going."

Taurus (April 21–May 21)—"Oh, you're a Taurus, full of bull and always trying to horn in."

Aries (March 21–April 20)—"Of course, the sign of the ram—always trying to ram their opinions down other people's throats."

Pisces (February 20–March 20) or Aquarius (January 21–February 17)—"Oh, sign of the fish. No wonder you seem all wet."

Although I haven't had the occasion to try all twelve of the signs yet, the ones I have used invariably got a laugh. And that's the name of the game.

A laugh turneth away wrath. Or at least it defuses the situation. It lets the bomb fizzle in the thrower's hands instead of exploding in your face.

A heckler makes the audience almost as nervous and jumpy as the speaker. If you get angry, you might push the crowd over to the side of their fellow member of the audience—the heckler. But that same embarrassed state can easily be turned into laughter. Make them laugh at *his* expense and they automatically come onto *your* side.

Recently the behavior of my two daughters brought to mind the old squelcher used by children. When my younger daughter calls her older sister "baby," she replies, "I know *you* are, but what am I?"

But the refrain indicates a classic strategy of the good retort. You assume the name-caller is describing himself. You let the obscenity stick to his dirty hands.

The Obscenity

Ever since Berkeley's Mario Savio discovered Anglo-Saxon, the four-letter word has become a popular speaker-taunting expletive.

I remember speaking in Illinois, where a student kept yelling at me "Mother ——."

To which I answered: "Glad to hear you're still around, Oedipus. You may know a friend of mine. Spiro Agnew. He's also Greek."

A variation of that is the cry "F—— off." Try the answer: "Hello, Portnoy. I see you have a complaint."

Another word in vogue is *sh*——. A possible retort is: "If your mother didn't toilet-train you, that's your problem, not mine."

Fascist Pig

If someone starts screaming Fascist or Nazi at you, say: "I could already guess your party registration, but aren't you wearing the wrong color shirt?"

Or listen to Tom Reed's reply to a congressional colleague: "I cannot hope to equal the volume of the voice of the gentleman from New York. This is equaled by the volume of what he does not know."

Hissing

For this type of loudmouth use the reply Ohio's Senator Tom Corwin once gave when he heard a heckler hissing him in the rear of an audience:

"There are only three things that hiss," said Tom, "a goose, a snake, and a fool—please identify yourself."

The Smart-Aleck Kid

One of the best squelches of a young heckler was made by Winston Churchill in his general election campaign of 1951.

The old man looked down at his adolescent tormenter and said, "I admire a manly man, and I rejoice in a womanly woman, but I cannot abide a boily boy."

When ex-President John Quincy Adams, in advanced years, was running for election to the House of Representatives, he was told by a young man in the audience, "Old man, why don't you shut up?"

And Adams replied, "An ass at twenty-five is older than a man at seventy-five."

In the 1960 campaign I did a series of street speeches in Philadelphia, sharing the platform of the back of a sound truck with a black lawyer named Cecil Moore. Moore, an old hand at dispersing hecklers, came to my rescue on more than one occasion.

Once he silenced a youngster by saying: "Does your mother know you're out this late?"

Another silencer he shot back was: "What's the matter, son, are you afraid I'm going to mention your father was a bachelor?"

The last exchange brings to mind the comeback Henry Clay once made in a speech when someone in the crowd yelled "Liar, liar" at him.

Replied Clay, "Now if you can give your name as well as your calling, we'd be glad to hear from you."

"Go to Hell"

In Pennsylvania, when a heckler assigned me that unheavenly route I answered,

"Look, I am speaking in Altoona today. Perhaps another day, I might consider speaking in *your* hometown."

Of course, I don't pretend to any great originality. I was only retreading the classic reply of Tom Reed, the one-time Republican Speaker of the House. When Reed, out on the campaign stump, received similarly profane directions, he said:

"Thank you. I've been speaking for many years, but this is the first time I have ever got invited to speak at the Democratic headquarters."

"Louder, Louder"

Occasionally you run across an audience clown who cries "Louder, louder" as if he wants to engage you in some sort of yelling match.

Benjamin Disraeli had the perfect retort for such a shouter: "Truth travels slowly, but it will even reach you in time."

General Rudeness and Ignorance

There are all sorts of one-liners politicians have used to squelch hecklers. Write them down on cards and have them ready if you are going to face a hostile audience.

Missouri's Senator George Vest once stopped the booing by saying:

"I feel like the Philistine in the Book of Judges who said he was just shot at by the jawbone of an ass."

And Speaker Tom Reed, quelling a noisy critic, said: "Some people never open their mouths without subtracting from the total sum of human knowledge."

Similarly, when British Prime Minister Harold Macmillan was once jeered, he retorted: "I have never found that criticism is ever inhibited by ignorance."

The best all-purpose line was given by Adlai Stevenson as he was heckled by some right-wingers in Dallas:

"I still believe," said Stevenson, "in the forgiveness of trespasses and the redemption of ignorance."

PART II

Ice-Breakers

TO MAKE FUN OF LONG-WINDEDNESS AND TO OPEN
BRIEF AND INFORMAL REMARKS

1   *Not having a prepared speech today, I feel like the soldier
from Fort Knox* who, with his girl friend, hurried into a judge's
office in my county one afternoon and asked the judge to marry
them.

"Got a license?" he asked.

"No, Judge," said the would-be bride. "John just got out for
weekend leave and the clerk's office is already closed."

"Sorry," said the judge, "I can't do it. Come back on Monday
and we'll have the ceremony."

"But, Judge," pleaded the girl, "John is just here for two days.
He is being shipped overseas at 8:00 A.M. Monday morning."

"I'm sorry, I can't help you," said the judge. "I can't marry you
without a license."

"But, Judge," said the not-to-be-downed soldier, "couldn't you
say just a few words to tide us over the weekend?"

(Although we don't have that kind of activity planned, I am
going to say a few words to tide us over while we . . .)

2   *I'm not going to be long tonight.* I don't want to be accused of what Senator Blackburn of Kentucky once said of a colleague. He was lolling in his chair in the Senate, trying not to listen
to a windy senator venting his wrath on big business. Noting the
disgusted look on the faces of the few colleagues who were listening, the speaker stopped and asked, "I trust, Mr. President, I am
not unduly trespassing on the time of this Senate?"

That was too much for Blackburn. He was on his feet in an instant, shouting, "There is a great difference between trespassing on time and encroaching on eternity!"

(So tonight I don't intend to encroach on eternity—I just want to deliver a simple message . . .)

3   *Remembering what Thomas Edison once said, I'm going to keep* my remarks brief. He was the guest at a dinner, and the chairman introduced the inventor with a long account of his inventions. He talked about the marvelous talking machine, as the phonograph was then known. Finally he sat down.

Edison arose and began his talk: "I thank the chairman for his kind remarks, but I must make one correction. God invented the talking machine. I only invented the first one that can be shut off."

(And I assure you that I am going to turn this machine off soon . . .)

4   *I plan to be brief because I know there is nothing more agonizing* than a long speech at a time like this. It brings to mind what a condemned man said back at the turn of the century in Dodge City. Just as the hanging was about to take place, a candidate for Congress shoved his way through the crowd to a place near the gallows.

As the sheriff was adjusting the rope, he said to the hanging victim, "You have ten minutes to live. Perhaps you would like to say something to the crowd."

The prisoner shook his head, sullenly indicating that he would not like to say anything. Whereupon the congressional aspirant jumped up on the gallows, opened his coat, and cried, "If the gentleman does not want his ten minutes and will kindly yield to me, I should like to begin by saying, if elected to Congress, I . . ."

That was too much for the prisoner. "Sheriff," he said, "I came here to be hung, not tortured. Pull the rope! . . ."—and they did.

(Well, I don't propose to torture anyone with a long speech; I only want to stress a few points . . .)

5   *As I begin my remarks, I want to remind myself of the warning* Adlai Stevenson gave when initiating a commencement speech:

"It is my job today as speaker to talk. It's your job as the audience to listen. If you get finished before I do, please feel free to get up and leave."

TO FOLLOW A FLATTERING INTRODUCTION

6   *That generous introduction reminds me a little of a story* that they tell about a farmer friend of mine back in upstate Pennsylvania who was taking a little white-face Hereford calf down a country road on the end of a rope. He was having some difficulty in making headway. He came to a little bridge over a shallow creek, with a dry creek bed, and the calf wouldn't move forward. He was tugging on the rope when a man drove up behind him in a car. The car couldn't pass because of the calf in the road, so the driver thought he would urge him on, and let out a loud blast on the horn. The calf responded by jumping sideways, over the edge of the bridge, and fell down in the creek bed.

The man walked up to where the farmer stood looking at the calf, and saw that the calf had fallen and broken its neck. It was dead, and the driver didn't know what to say.

Finally the farmer looked up and said, "Well, stranger, I appreciate your intentions, but don't you think that was an awfully loud toot for such a little calf?"

(And similarly it was an awfully loud toot of an introduction for someone as inadequate as I feel as I look at this audience . . .)

7   *Thank you for that all too generous introduction.* If, as Mark Twain said, a man can live a month on one compliment, the chairman has just assured me of immortality. But he will go to heaven for his charity unless he goes somewhere else for his exaggerations.

8   *Thank you, thank you for those nice words*—but I always caution myself to remember what Adlai Stevenson once said about a flattering introduction. He said, "Praise is like perfume—all right to smell it as long as you don't swallow it."

9   *Thank you for that applause.* As Bishop Fulton Sheen once said, "Applause sums up the highest of Christian virtues. To applaud, as you just did, at the beginning of the speech, is an act of

faith. And if you applaud in the middle of my speech, it is an act of hope. But if you applaud at the end of my speech, it is an act of charity."

10   *The only way I can describe such an introduction* is that it is pure euphemism—you know—perfumed language. The best way to define that is to tell you what a friend of my grandfather's once did when he had to fill out an application for an insurance policy. One of the questions he had to answer was, "How old was your father when he died, and of what did he die?"

The problem was that his father had been hanged, but he did not want to put that on his application. He puzzled over it for quite a while. Finally he wrote, "My father was sixty-five when he died. He came to his end while participating in a public function when the platform gave way."

(But however euphemistic the introduction, I am glad to be participating in this function . . .)

11   *I thank the chairman for all those nice things he said about me.* You know the people of this city are always very kind. The last time I was here a number of ladies came up and told me I had made a good speech. They are so courteous out here. Whether they are genuinely sincere about it or not, they at least tell you you do all right.

One elderly lady the last time was particularly nice. She told me this speech was so good that it should be printed. I said, "It won't be printed anywhere that I know of." She was so insistent that it had to be published that I told her: "Perhaps it will someday, posthumously."

And she replied, "I hope it will be soon."

(Whenever my demise, I can assure you what I say today will not ever be published posthumously or even "prehumously" . . .)

12   *I thank you for the generous introduction.* The people here are always so kind. I will never forget the great kindness the chairman did for me. He has done many nice things for me. When I was a speaker out here a short time ago at a men's meeting, several people came up to tell me I had made a good speech, but one fellow came up with real blood in his eye. "You know," he said, "that was the lousiest speech I have ever heard."

And that is a little disconcerting. The chairman of the dinner was right there at my side. He knew this fellow; he was a mutual friend of his and mine. He completely set my mind at rest and made me feel wonderful. He said: "Listen, don't pay any attention to that fellow. He is a moron and he repeats everything he hears."

(Well, the moral is you can't believe everything you hear and that holds true for the introduction you just heard . . .)

13   *When you mention that I am a public official with high responsibility,* I think of the other day when I was in the capital doing an errand at one of the agencies for an aggrieved citizen. I drove down and looked for a parking place. Places reserved for officials were all used. So I parked in a "no parking" zone. Under the windshield wiper, I left a note:

"I drove around the block five times—no space. I have a public duty to do for my constituents or else I'll lose my job. (Signed) Forgive us our trespasses."

When I returned, there was a parking ticket—and also a note: "I've been on this beat five years. I have a duty to do for the people or else I'll lose my job. (Signed) Lead us not into temptation."

(I hope that what I say today is going to lead no one astray . . .)

14   *I thank you for that kind introduction, but I must confess that* tenure of public office automatically does not imply any such endowment of special ability or talent. I remember the exchange a United States senator had with a representative from an Indian reservation back in the 1920's. The Indian, who was from Oklahoma, was testifying before a Senate Committee on Indian Affairs: "I have come before you, gentlemen," said the Indian, "to plead for the right of my tribe to manage its own lands."

"I object," said the senator, "on the ground that the average Indian hasn't the intelligence to manage property."

"Why, Senator, do you think I haven't that much sense?" asked the Indian representative.

"I said the *average* Indian," said the senator. "You surely can't be average. Your tribe undoubtedly would send the smartest man they had to plead their case."

"That isn't so, sir," said the Indian. "We Indians are just like the people of the United States. We never send our smartest men to Congress."

(Now that I have warned you about the limitations of my qualifications, I feel free to begin my remarks . . .)

15   *Every time I am introduced as "Honorable,"* I think of the Kentucky colonel who was called to testify in a case in Louisville. This was after World War II, and a leading Washington lawyer who had been a cabinet officer was trying the case. A key witness for the other side was a man of substance and esteem whose membership in the establishment is best described by the fact that he was called "Colonel."

Now, of course, the Colonel in his title was strictly honorary and the lawyer, in trying to discredit his testimony, said, "Now, before you testify, will you tell just what the 'Colonel' before your name signifies?"

The old colonel replied: "Counselor, it's just like the 'honorable' before your name—it doesn't mean a darn thing."

(But even if my superannuated title doesn't mean a thing, it does mean a lot to be invited to address a group which does have great distinction . . .)

Ice-Breakers

TO TOUCH ON THE WARMTH, HOSPITALITY, OR
REPUTATION OF THE HOST ORGANIZATION

16   *To be invited back to speak a second time is always a great honor.* It shows how generous and kind you people are. As you know, a return engagement is not always automatic. I remember when Winston Churchill received an invitation from George Bernard Shaw to one of his opening plays back in the early 1900's.

The note read: "Enclosed are two tickets to the first-night performance of a play of mine. Bring a friend—if you have one."

Churchill sent back this reply: "Dear G.B.S.: I thank you very much for the invitation and tickets. Unfortunately, I am engaged on that night, but could I have tickets for the second night—if there is one."

(And so I am proud that there is one for me—a second night. But this is probably more a tribute to charity than to any popularity.)

17   *Although I have given more than a few speeches, this is one of* the few times a group has had me back again. Some organizations, like people, often don't want a thing a second time.

For example, a friend of mine not long ago found himself in London on one of those foggy nights—and went to a club where he had reciprocal membership. Hoping to strike up a conversation with a distinguished-looking Englishman sitting nearby, he said, "May I buy you a drink?"

"No," said the Britisher coolly. "Don't drink. Tried it once and didn't like it."

My friend ordered himself a drink and after a while he thought he'd try to make conversation again—so he said, "Would you like one of my cigars?"

"No. Don't smoke. Tried tobacco once and didn't like it."

That stopped my friend, but then after a bit he thought, surely the gentleman would not be adverse to playing some rummy, so he asked him to join him in a game.

"No. Don't like card games. Tried it once and didn't like it. But my son will be dropping by after a bit. Perhaps he'll join you."

My American friend settled back in his chair and said: "Your only son, I presume!"

(So I'm glad you had the tolerance and fortitude to try me a second time . . .)

18   *When I think of your organization, certain things automatically come to mind.* It's like an association test a cagy old Church of England dean once gave to a young man who was hoping to win a church-endowed scholarship to Oxford. The Dean was known as a strict teetotaler, and he started off with the word "Gordon," hoping to trick the lad into making the wrong association—like that which rhymes with sin and goes with tonic.

"What does Gordon make you think of, young man?"

And the young man replied, "Gordon—I think of General Gordon, the great colonial statesman in the Sudan."

And the Dean said, "Haig, Haig—what does that make you think of?"

"Lord Haig—the distinguished marshal and commander of the Allies in World War I."

Then the Dean, making one last attempt to catch the student, said, "What does VAT 69 make you think of?"

The student thought for a moment and said, "Isn't that the Pope's telephone number?"

(Well, there is no ambiguity about what the name of your organization stands for in the minds of people . . .)

19   *We all have our own ideas of man's best friend.* I know the choice of a friend of mine who recently took a vacation mountain-climbing the Alps with a native Swiss guide. On the windy, snowy slopes, my friend and guide temporarily lost their bearings for a bit and in the bitter cold were preparing camp when all at once they sighted the familiar Saint Bernard dog trotting along with a keg tied around its neck.

The Swiss guide said, "Here comes man's best friend."

"Yes," said the American, "and look at the big furry dog that's bringing it."

(That may be one view of man's best friend, but I know some who will testify that this organization certainly has been a great friend . . .)

20   *At the reception earlier tonight I again had the experience of enjoying your warm welcome and outgoing hospitality.* In fact, I might characterize you by the phrase once used to describe a former senator.

Back in the 1950 senatorial primary campaign in Florida, veteran Claude Pepper was opposed by George Smathers. Pepper was especially strong in the "Bible belt," or northern, section of Florida. To shake the hold Pepper had on these people, Smathers developed a special speech making use of the facts that Pepper, a Harvard Law School graduate, has a niece who was a staff member of a Senate Subcommittee, and a sister who acted in New York.

For the county courthouse rallies, Smathers would say, "Are you aware, my friends, that in his youth Claude Pepper was found —matriculating—in Harvard, that before marriage he habitually indulged in—celibacy. Not only that, he has practiced—nepotism —in Washington with his own niece; and he has a sister who is a —thespian—in wicked Greenwich Village in New York. Worst of all, my friends, Claude Pepper is known all over Washington for his latent tendency toward overt extraversion."

(Well, ladies and gentlemen, after attending the reception tonight, I think I can say there is nothing latent about your "overt extraversion" . . .)

21   *I am very happy to be here tonight with a group that I feel most comfortable and at home with.* I certainly don't feel like William Allen White did in 1928. White was attending a Democratic convention as a reporter. Senator James Reed was scheduled to open the proceedings. As he stood at the rostrum, Reed looked around and found there was no minister present to open the proceedings with a prayer, but he did notice White, a Republican, seated in the press gallery. So he said: "Gentlemen, since there are no ministers present, I shall call on my good friend, William Allen White, to open the convention with prayer."

White, boiling mad, strode to the podium and said, "Ladies and gentlemen, you will have to excuse me. You see, I am a little out of my element, and the fact is, I prefer the Lord does not know that I am here."

(Well, ladies and gentlemen, I can say that I feel very much in my element here, and I'm glad that the Lord does know I'm here . . .)

22   *I must say, for one who has come to your city for the first time,* how warm the reception and welcome has been. Certainly I do not feel the way Andrew Carnegie reportedly once felt when he returned to his native Scotland to visit some of the towns of his childhood. In one he visited a kirk and after the service the minister told Carnegie that he was asking for contributions for a new stained-glass window. Carnegie immediately offered to send a thousand dollars to the fund.

A week later, Carnegie heard the minister in the kirk give a sermon on charity and gave as an example the generosity of Andrew Carnegie, who gave ten thousand dollars. Afterward, Carnegie sought out the parson to correct the mistake. But the minister said, "You would not want to disappoint all those people now by only giving one thousand dollars."

Carnegie agreed to give the ten thousand, but on one condition

—that an inscription from the Bible be put under the window when finished. When it was done, the minister asked what the verse was that he wanted.

Carnegie cited Matthew, chapter 25, verse 43: When the minister opened his Bible and read the selected verse, it read: "I was a stranger and ye took me not in."

(Well, ladies and gentlemen, I may have been a stranger but I have been most generously welcomed and taken in . . .)

23   *I have always had a high respect for your organization and the work that it has been doing.* I might say that my admiration for you is like what a gas-meter man in my town said not long ago under different circumstances.

A most attractive neighbor of mine decided to begin her household chores just after she had gotten her husband off to work. Still dressed in her housecoat, she spied above the washing machine in the basement a big spider in a cobweb. Afraid of getting the web in her hair, which she had just had done the day before, she grabbed the nearest means of protection—her son's football helmet—and with a baseball bat she slew the beast. Needing something to wrap up the remains, she took off her housecoat, scooped up the web and popped it in one motion into the washing machine. At that moment, the meter man appeared, looked at the woman in her altogether, with the baseball bat and football helmet, and said: "Lady, I don't know what sport you're trying to play, but whatever it is I'm sure rooting for your team."

(And knowing the great activities your society is actively engaged in, I am sure rooting for the success . . .)

24   *Over the past few years, I know of no group that has been more of a staunch friend than your organization.* You have been there in the pinch, when really needed. Of course, as I learned first as a Boy Scout, that's when you *really* need friends.

The Scoutmaster had taken a group of us out for our first overnight hike. Since there were lots of copperhead snakes in the region, the Scoutmaster gave us these instructions: "If any of you are bitten by a snake, immediately apply your mouth to the puncture and suck vigorously at the aperture."

At this point, one of my fellow Scouts said, "What happens, sir, if you get bitten on the backside?"

The Scoutmaster thought for a moment and then told us: " 'Tis then that you get to know your real friends."

(In a different way, I have come to know what a real friend your organization has been in the last few years . . .)

FOR BUSINESS GROUPS OR TRADE ASSOCIATIONS

25   *I am always happy to have the chance to speak to a group of businessmen such as yourselves,* because it is business that powers America—provides the jobs, builds the homes, and expands the economy. The profit motive is not something to condemn but commend. In that connection I recall a college reunion I attended not long ago. One grad who was remembered as the dimmest in the class returned in a chauffeured Rolls-Royce. It seems he had become a fabulously successful president of a gasket company. Naturally, all of us, his former classmates, were curious how one that stupid had made so much money. So after we plied him with lots of drinks, a friend of mine put the question to him.

"Just how were you able to put together this gasket operation you run?"

"It was easy," he replied. "I found a manufacturer who could make them at one cent apiece and then I sold them at five cents apiece. And you just can't beat that four percent profit."

(And I don't think you can beat the profit system anywhere for making a country economically stronger . . .)

26   *As one who believes wholeheartedly in the system of private* enterprise, I take great pride in speaking to your group today. There seems to be a new breed of Puritan today who thinks of the profit motive as the old variety thought of sex—something inherently evil instead of something natural and basic to economic growth. I recall a debate in the House of Commons years ago when a Laborite minister was extolling the benefits of socialism.

"Under the Socialist government more housing units have been built than ever before.

"Indeed under socialism it can be proved that more hospitals have been constructed than ever before.

"Not only that but it can be shown that more milk has been provided to English babies than ever before.

"As a matter of fact, under the Socialist government, we have witnessed the greatest increase in population in the history of the island."

At that moment, the great Winston Churchill reportedly interrupted: "Would the right honorable gentlemen concede that the last statistic is due to private enterprise?"

(And so I would say that the major role in the growth of America has been due to private enterprise . . .)

Doctors

27   *Members of the medical profession get more than their share of criticism.* They are often accused of burying their mistakes. I recall the story of the man who died and arrived at the gates of heaven. A messenger of Saint Peter took his name and disappeared. Later, the messenger came back and told the newly arrived applicant to heaven that he was very sorry but his name was not on the books. He was not registered to be received in heaven. The messenger suggested that he try hell.

The poor fellow made his way to the gates of hell and was promptly interviewed by a representative of Satan. Here again he was informed that he was not on the books and not registered to be admitted to hell. It was suggested that he return to heaven once more.

The fellow, now thoroughly confused, returned to the pearly gates and announced that his name had not been found on the register in hell and that Satan had suggested that he try heaven again. The fellow was taken to the office outside the gates, and Saint Peter himself carefully checked every name again. Suddenly, the name was discovered far down the list.

Saint Peter turned to him and said, "There seems to have been a mistake here. Someone made an error. You are not due to arrive in heaven for six more years. Who is your doctor?"

(I can say from all the doctors I have known that lives have been lengthened. Certainly the life expectancy in this country has been measurably increased . . .)

Lawyers

28 *I have always had a great respect for lawyers of this bar* —for their astuteness and skill. I recall some years ago a senior partner of a very prestigious law firm in this city was representing the defense against a plaintiff—an old lady who was suing an airline for injuries suffered coming off the airplane platform steps. But as the case came up for trial, it ran right into his scheduled vacation in Miami, so he turned the case over to a junior associate. One day when he got back from the beach, the hotel clerk handed him a telegram. It was from his associate and it read, "Justice has prevailed."

Somewhat distressed, he immediately called Western Union and sent a wire to his junior associate. It read, "Appeal at once."

(Seriously, I know that justice and passionate respect for the rights of others is a distinguishing quality of all lawyers and especially the members of this bar . . .)

29 *Back in Pennsylvania, the man on the street has clear regard for lawyers, their worth and merit.* I recall two farmers who were quarreling about the location of the boundary between their adjoining farms. One said, "If you don't concede that my boundary is located where I say, I will bring a suit against you in court." The other replied, "That's all right. I'll be there when the case is tried." The first said, "If I lose the case, I'll appeal to the Supreme Court of Pennsylvania." The other said, "All right, I'll be there when that appeal is heard." Then the first one said, "If I lose that case in the Supreme Court of Pennsylvania, I'll appeal to the Supreme Court of the United States." The second one said, "That's all right; I'll be there when that appeal is heard." And then the first one said, "Well, then if I lose that case in the Supreme Court of the United States, I'll take it straight to hell." The second one said, "I won't be there, but my lawyer will."

(Well, I won't go that far but I will say that lawyers are there when you need them in the hottest of fights . . .)

Religious Organizations

30   *As a Protestant, I suppose I should feel out of place addressing* a Catholic group. But I don't think it matters what church you go to, as long as you go—all churches do the work of the Lord. I recall the famous exchange between the Archbishop of Canterbury and the British head of the Catholic Church, Cardinal Hensley, in London over a century ago. Coming out of a meeting they had just attended together, the archbishop offered the cardinal a ride in his carriage. After all, said the Anglican archbishop, "We both are engaged in God's work."

"Yes," the cardinal replied, "You in your way, and I in His!"

(Well, I may be no theologian, but I know the type of work your organization does, and surely your work must be His work . . .)

31   *It's like old home week being here speaking to fellow Presbyterians.* This is the faith of my fathers and where I got my religion. When I think of a church such as this, I think of a lady back in my home town who was one of those Pentecostal types. She took a trip to England and went to church on Sunday morning at Westminster Abbey. Here were the clergy in all their robes and all the pomp and all the ceremony, and she didn't think she would hear anything that would remind her of her own revivalist heritage. But when the clergyman got up, after all the kneeling and standing and the liturgy, he began to preach from the Bible.

Well, that quite amazed her, and he said a few things which she agreed with, and she said, "Amen, brother!" This of course shook the congregation, and the minister almost lost his train of thought. He said something else she agreed with and she said, "Preach it, brother!"

Finally, an usher came and tapped her on the shoulder and said, "Madam, you can't do that in here."

"But," she said, "I have got religion."

"Yes," he replied, "but you didn't get it here."

(Well, I am proud to say that I did get my religion here . . .)

Women

32   *When I think about the role women play,* I think of what former Prime Minister Menzies of Australia said when he was sworn into office and various representatives of the press were on hand to interview him.

The reporter from the radical press said, somewhat bluntly, "I suppose, Mr. Prime Minister, that you will consult the powerful interests that control you in choosing your cabinet?"

"Young man," snapped the Prime Minister, "I would ask that you keep my wife's name out of this."

(Well, I am not fool enough to believe that wives can be kept out of anything . . .)

33   *I often think we don't appreciate all our women do for us.* I agree with what Joseph Choate said when ambassador to the Court of St. James. He was called to make a toast to the Pilgrim Fathers at the annual Pilgrim Dinner in London. He paid tribute to those brave Massachusetts settlers who withstood the rigor of New England winters and the terror of Indian raids and the pangs of hunger.

"But let us give thought," he added, "to the Pilgrim Mothers who not only had to endure everything the Pilgrim Fathers endured, but—remember this—they also had to endure the Pilgrim Fathers."

34   *It is always a pleasure to follow a lady on the rostrum.* I recall what "Uncle Joe" Cannon said some years ago during a lengthy debate with a lady member of the House. Uncle Joe, then in his eighties, arose, and asked, "Will the lady yield?" When the lady continued to hold the floor, he asked again, "Will the distinguished lady please yield?"

Finally she replied with a smile, "The lady will be delighted to yield to the gentleman from Illinois."

The aged Cannon replied, "My God! Now that she has finally yielded, what can I do about it?"

(Well, I guess I can say you have yielded me some sort of opportunity in letting me speak today . . .)

Youth

35   *As I look at the young people who make up this audience, I think* of how in only a few years you who are today's students will be tomorrow's shapers of our society. Your future role recalls the story about the late Sir Winston Churchill.

It was in 1959, when Churchill was at the sunset of his life. He was accustomed to spending most of his time in the antechambers where they dispensed liquid refreshments. On one occasion, the bell rang for a division vote, and Churchill, thoroughly fortified, began to wobble toward the door as the 250-pound Laborite from Liverpool, Bessie Braddock, came waddling toward the same door. There was the inevitable collision, and down went Bessie for the count.

Furious, Bessie got herself off the floor and said, "Sir Winston, you are drunk. Furthermore, you are disgustingly drunk."

Churchill looked at the obese Bessie and replied, "Mrs. Braddock, you are ugly. Furthermore, you are disgustingly ugly. What's more, tomorrow I, Winston Churchill, shall be sober."

(So today you may be the students, but tomorrow will find you assuming the leadership in all walks of society . . .)

TO UNDERSCORE THE SPEAKER'S EXPERTISE
OR OBJECTIVITY ON A SUBJECT

36   *When I accepted the invitation to speak tonight, your chairman and* I discussed what should be the subject of my address. All kinds of topics were suggested, but I am happy to say he let me pick a subject with which I have some familiarity. It reminds me of when I was back in college, and had signed up for a snap course called "New Testament Survey," taught by an old minister. For years his final exam question was the same: "Describe and Trace the Travels of the Apostle Paul."

Naturally, everybody committed to memory a detailed answer to that question. The year I took it, the professor surprised everyone by handing out a different exam question: "Discuss and Criticize the Sermon on the Mount." Everybody walked out except for one football guard, "Tiny," who was surely the densest member of the class.

When we came back from vacation, we looked at the posted marks. All failed except Tiny, who barely passed. When we asked him what happened, he said he wrote: "Who am I to criticize the words of the Master? But I would like to tell about the travels of the Apostle Paul."

(Tonight, I would like to talk about something which I do know about . . .)

37   *A good speech, I heard once, offers facts, not furor.* It should enlighten the situation, as Abraham Lincoln once explained. In the Civil War Lincoln was disturbed by people who pretended to be wise on a minimum diet of facts. They offered wisdom they did not possess. Lincoln told the story of a backwoods traveler lost in a terrific thunderstorm. The rider floundered through the mud until his horse gave out. Then he stood alone in the middle of the road while lightning streaked and thunder roared around him. One crash seemed to shake the earth underneath, and it brought the traveler to his knees. He cried out, "O Lord, I'm not a praying man, but I'll make the prayer brief and to the point: If it's all the same to you, give us a little more light and a little less noise."

(So let us today try to add some light to a subject that has been noised about by so much controversy lately . . .)

38   *Too often we are misled by catching only one side of the subject.* Like the wife of a friend of mine who went along with her husband to attend a business meeting in Phoenix. While her husband was tied up in meetings all morning, she slept late. Upon waking, she took a dip in the swimming pool. Afterward, wanting to have a good look at the city, she went up to the roof. The warm Arizona sun was so nice that she decided to lie down and catch some of it. After a while, seeing there was no one around, she took off her two-piece suit and lay down on her stomach and covered her backside with the bath towel. For some time she lay there when suddenly a hotel clerk appeared, all agitated and upset.

"Madam, you must come down at once. This is an indecent situation."

"What do you mean—there could only be planes that see me here—anyway, I'm covered with a towel."

"Madam, don't you realize you are lying over our dining room skylight?"

(Well, today we are going to look at both sides of the problem . . .)

TO INTRODUCE A PROGRAM OR A PLAN

39   *It is important to have an objective—to know where you are going.* I recall what my old Presbyterian minister said one time when he was quizzed by a Lutheran pastor about his theology.

The Lutheran asked my minister: "Don't you believe in predestination?"

"Well, yes, in a way."

"Don't you believe in foreordainment?"

"Well, yes, in a way."

"Well, I suppose if you knew as a Presbyterian you were going to hell, you'd accept it?"

"I'd rather be a Presbyterian knowing I am going to hell than a Lutheran not knowing where the hell I am going."

(So today I want to start out by examining just where we are going . . .)

40   *One of the worst excuses a man can make for a policy gone wrong is to say there was no other way.* The highest responsibility for a decision-maker is to examine all alternatives. We remember the story about Winston Churchill who at a reception in Australia in the 1950's found himself next to the stiff-necked, teetotaler Methodist Bishop of Melbourne. An attractive, buxom girl appeared with a tray offering first to the British prime minister a drink, which he took, and then to the Methodist bishop. The bishop was aghast at the alcoholic offer: "Young lady, I'd rather commit adultery than take an intoxicating beverage."

Thereupon, Sir Winston said, "Come back here, lass; I didn't know we had a choice."

(And today I might say we also have a choice in the direction we are going to go . . .)

41   *Most speeches offer programs; mine tonight will be no exception.* Now audiences naturally want to be aware of all the implications that might arise from the adoption of the program. The effects, I can assure you, will be far better than those foreseen in an incident in the English Parliament two hundred years ago. At the time of our War of Independence, there was a rebellious member of the House of Commons named John Wilkes. Now Wilkes took delight in supporting the American cause, much to the consternation of the Tory government. Wilkes's reputation for demagoguery was only exceeded by his reputation for general debauchery.

One day, after a speech that seemed treasonable to the Tory hierarchy, Wilkes found himself attacked by a member of the front bench, Lord Sandwich.

Said Lord Sandwich: "The honorable gentleman from Middlesex will have a limited career in this chamber, for it shall either end on the gallows or by a loathsome disease."

Wilkes coolly replied: "The honorable Lord may well be correct. It all depends on whether I embrace his programs or embrace his mistress."

(Well, tonight although I don't have any mistress for you to embrace, I do have a program . . .)

TO SERVE AS A PRELUDE TO A REQUEST
FOR A CONTRIBUTION OR HELP

42   *A successful conclusion to my talk tonight depends not on me but on you.* But I know you have the concern, compassion and commitment to do it. None of you could be characterized as three brothers I recently heard about. They were the children of a hardworking couple back home who had struggled for thirty years, sacrificing themselves for their three sons whom they put through college. Never once did they take a vacation. Now they wanted to take a trip to Florida, and they asked their sons for some money. The first son was a lawyer, and he said, "No, I can't do it. I'm

just fitting out a new law office and sending my son to an expensive camp."

So they asked their second son, a doctor. But he said, "No, I'm sorry I can't. I've just bought a new house, and my wife is putting in a new kitchen."

Then they asked the third son, who was an engineer. He replied: "It just would be impossible for me to do it. I have just bought a big boat for the family and am remodeling our summer home on the lake."

Finally the father pleaded, "Look, we have worked all our lives —not one day of vacation. We never had any money saved except that saved for your education. In fact, do you realize that your mother and I were so busy working trying to save money that we never took the time out to get a marriage license?"

"Father," said all the three sons in unison, "Do you realize what that makes us?"

"Yes," said the father, "and cheap ones, too."

(But I know we have no cheap ones in the audience to-night . . .)

43   *I'm going to ask for your help tonight.* Now there is a right way and a wrong way to help. For an example of the wrong way, consider the young wife of an older businessman I heard about. He was a widower who married a very buxom young nightclub singer many years his junior. Shortly after the honeymoon, the husband suffered a serious heart attack.

When the young bride visited her sick mate in the hospital, she found him in an oxygen tent in the intensive care unit. The husband said to her, "Don't worry, dear. I have amply provided for you. The house, in both our names, will revert to you. And you know that all the stocks and bonds will go to you, meaning a principal of over two million."

"Oh, darling," cried the girl, "I am so worried about you. Is there anything I can do to help?"   ·

"Yes," he replied, "would you mind taking your hand off the oxygen tube?"

(Yes, there is a right way for you to help . . .)

44   *All of you people here look like generous people and I know you are* going to follow the advice a model gave to a friend

of mine. This friend—who has recently become single again—was going to be in Los Angeles for an extended trip and so he asked a mutual friend of ours for a few good phone numbers. The evening after he landed, he called this gorgeous redhead model named Monica who lived in Bel Air. She said she was delighted and gave him explicit directions on how to reach her apartment.

"When you get to the Bel Air Plaza, take the lobby elevator to the seventh floor—turn left and look for 718. When you reach my apartment, use your right elbow to ring the buzzer. When I hear that, I can release the security catch. All you have to do is put your left shoulder to the door and kick the bottom with your right foot."

"Look," said my friend, "What do you mean with all the directions calling for an elbow, shoulder, and foot?"

"But surely, darling," said Monica, "you aren't going to come in empty-handed?"

TO REFER TO THE PREDICAMENT OR CONFUSED SITUATION THAT SOCIETY FINDS ITSELF IN

45   *I know all of you have an idea from the newspaper of just how critical conditions are.* But I want to say that it is even worse than what you have read. It is like what my son said not long ago.

Now it is the custom in our family at Sunday dinner to ask what the children learned in Sunday School. So, one day I asked my boy what the lesson was that day, and he said Moses and the fleeing Israelites.

"What did you find out about them?" I asked.

"Well," said the boy, "there were these Israelites and they were trying to escape from the bad Egyptians—and the Egyptians chased them right to the Red Sea."

"Yes, and then what happened?"

"Well, Moses took out his walkie-talkie and said, 'Chief Engineer, build the pontoon.' And then over the pontoon the Israelites went."

"Really, and then what?"

"Well, the Egyptians started to come over the pontoon, too, and so Moses picked up the walkie-talkie again and said, 'Chief Engineer, dynamite the pontoon,' and the Egyptians went down in the ocean."

Then I said, "Now are you sure that's the way the teacher told the story to you?"

"Well, Daddy, if you'd heard the story the way the Sunday School teacher told it, you'd never believe it."

(And if I told you about the actual conditions today, you'd never believe it . . .)

46   *The situation which suggests the title of my speech today* reminds me of the time a few years ago when I was attending a conference. I went to the hotel desk to check for messages, and I noted the harried state of the desk clerk. I asked him what was wrong and he said he had been on the phone with a guest. The guest, who had obviously been imbibing, had asked in a wobbly voice, "What time does the bar open?"

And the desk clerk had said, "Eleven A.M."

Sometime later the drunk called again. "Say, what time did you say the bar opened?"

Again the clerk said, "Eleven A.M."

A third time the clerk answered the inebriated guest's ring. "Say, can you tell me again what time the bar opens?" Exasperated, the clerk said, "Listen, you're a pest. In your state, we won't allow you to get in."

"Hell," he answered, "I don't want to get in. I've been all night locked up in the bar—I want to get out."

(Today we want to explore ways of extricating ourselves from a bad situation . . .)

47   *Now when we look at some of the problems we face today,* a lot of us like to look to Congress as the source of our troubles instead of looking at ourselves. We recall the famous Chaplain of the Senate, Dr. Edward Hale, was asked the question:

"Doctor, when you pray as Chaplain of the Senate, do you look at the tragic condition of the country and the many problems existing in the country and then pray that the Almighty will give the senators the wisdom with which to resolve those problems?"

And Dr. Hale replied, "No. I do not look at the country and pray for the senators. I look at the senators and then pray for the country."

(Today let us look at the country and pray for ourselves . . .)

48 *The situation that prompts my speech could, I suppose,* be blamed on politicians who lacked foresight or courage. It recalls the classic story of how an engineer, doctor, and politician were discussing which was the oldest profession. The doctor said the oldest profession was his. "You see, it was a surgical operation that made Eve out of Adam's rib."

But the engineer replied, "Yes, but it was the engineer who brought the world out of the chaos."

Then replied the politician, "But who do you think created the chaos?"

(Well, the chaos or mess we find ourselves in today may not be completely the fault of politicians . . .)

49 *There are those who think society today holds out little hope of improvement.* Their judgment is not unlike that made by a British admiral years ago of an Anglican bishop. The two had gone to school at Eton before World War I. Both were brilliant students, bitter in their rivalry; both went on to great success. One became distinguished as an admiral in the Royal Navy; the other a ranking bishop of the Church of England. Though many years passed, their hate for each other remained undiminished. Years later they encountered each other in London's Liverpool Street station. The bishop went over to the admiral in his dark blue uniform and all his braid, and spoke haughtily.

"I say, Conductor, which is the next train to Manchester?"

The admiral, looking at the portly bishop in his belted clerical cassock replied, "Madam, in your condition, I shouldn't think you would be going anywhere."

(Gentlemen, with the condition we find society in today, we might wonder where we are going . . .)

50 *We meet tonight in common awareness that time is growing short*—that what remains to be done has to be done quickly if it is to be done at all. In the spirit of that urgency, we recall the cry of Prime Minister Sir Winston Churchill when he was on his way to America on the *Queen Mary* in 1953. In the majestic main saloon after dinner, he and his party were being served brandy. Churchill asked his science adviser, Lord Cherwell, whether all the liquor he had consumed in his life would fill the hall. Cherwell took out the slide rule he always carried with him, and after some calculation on paper, told Churchill and the party that his combined liquor consumption would fill the saloon about to Churchill's nose.

Sir Winston, seeming a bit disappointed, reflected a bit and then said, "When I look at the high expanses of this hall and then think of my seventy-nine years, I can only say how much there is left to do and how little time there is to do it."

(So today we have much to do and little time . . .)

Mind-Wakers

Action

see ADVENTURE, INVOLVEMENT;
also APATHY

51   The frontiersman fighter Davy Crockett carried with him a watch-chain seal given to him by a friend. The seal's motto read "Be always sure you're right—then go ahead."

52   In World War I, British Admiral Beatty received a radiogram from another admiral: "Scarborough being shelled. I am proceeding toward Hull." Lord Beatty wired his reply: "Are you? I am going to Scarborough."

53   At the Congress of Vienna, Prince de Ligne made this comment about the diplomatic maneuverings: "They dance, but nothing happens."

54   Man is a fighting animal, his thoughts are his banners, and it is a failure of nerve in him if they are only thoughts.—*George Santayana*

55   I intend to go in harm's way.—*John Paul Jones*

56   An overly cautious pupil of Confucius used to think three times before committing himself to anything. On hearing of this Confucius told him, "Two times is enough."

Adventure

see ACTION, INVOLVEMENT

57   There is a calculated risk in everything; there has been a calculated risk in every stage of American development. The na-

tion was built by men who took risks—pioneers who were not afraid of failure, scientists who were not afraid of truth, thinkers who were not afraid of progress, dreamers who were not afraid of action.—*Brooks Atkinson*

58   The timorous may stay at home.—*Benjamin Cardozo*

59   The great achievements of the past were the adventures of the past. Only the adventurous can understand the greatness of the past.—*Alfred North Whitehead*

Age

see also YOUTH

60   A man in overalls was sitting on a bench reading the sports page outside the Supreme Court. A reporter who was supposed to interview Justice Oliver Wendell Holmes on his eighty-seventh birthday asked the bench occupant what he thought of him.

"Holmes—" the mechanic said. "Oh, sure, he's the young judge on the Supreme Court that's always disagreeing with the old guys."

61   Immanuel Kant wrote his *Anthropology* at seventy-four; Verdi composed his opera *Otello* at seventy-four; and Titian painted his historic "Battle of Lepanto" at ninety-eight!

62   Old man, perennial recruit of crisis, not detached from enterprises, feeling the approach of the eternal cold, but never weary of staring into the shadows watchful for the gleam of hope.—*Charles de Gaulle*

America

see HERITAGE, PATRIOTISM, UNITY

63   General Eisenhower, in June 1945, after World War II, spoke in the Guildhall in London. His point in that speech can be summed up by one of his sentences about his faith in America and the democratic way of life:

"I hope you believe we proved the doubters wrong."

64   British scientist Thomas Huxley visited Johns Hopkins University in 1910 and said about America:
"It has great potential, but what are you going to do with it?"

65   In 1793 the French writer Jean de Crèvecoeur asked a famous question:
"What then is the American? This new man?"

66   As John Gunther wrote in *Inside America,* ours is the only country deliberately founded on a "good idea."

67   The American Revolution was a beginning, not a consummation.—*Woodrow Wilson*

68   To every man his chance, to every man regardless of his birth, his shining, golden opportunity. To every man the right to live, to work, to be himself and to become whatever things his manhood and his vision can combine to make him. This . . . is the promise of America.—*Thomas Wolfe*

69   We need some great statements about what America is about and what we can do about it.—*Theodore M. Hesburgh*

70   Americanism is a question of principle, of idealism, of character: it is not a matter of birthplace or creed or line of descent.
—*Theodore Roosevelt*

71   We talk about the American Dream, and want to tell the world about the American Dream, but what is that Dream, in most cases, but the dream of material things? I sometimes think that the United States for this reason is the greatest failure the world has ever seen.—*Eugene O'Neill*

72   America is much more than a geographical fact. It is a political and moral fact—the first community in which men set out in principle to institutionalize freedom, responsible government, and human equality.—*Adlai Stevenson*

73   There are those, I know, who will reply that the liberation of humanity, the freedom of man and mind is nothing but a dream. They are right. It is the American Dream.—*Archibald MacLeish*

74   In the American design each group in our nation has spe-

cial problems. None has special rights. Each has peculiar needs. None has peculiar privileges.—*Dwight D. Eisenhower*

75   America has believed that in differentiation, not in uniformity, lies the path of progress.—*Louis Brandeis*

76   Eager, solicitous, hungry, rabid, busy-bodied America: catch thy breath and correct thyself.—*Ralph Waldo Emerson*

77   We Americans are the peculiar, chosen people—the Israel of our time—we bear the ark of liberties of the world.—*Herman Melville*

78   The greatness of America lies not in being more enlightened than any other nation, but rather in her ability to repair her faults.—*Alexis de Tocqueville*

79   America is a young country with an old mentality.—*George Santayana*

80   We are now at the point where we must decide whether we are to honor the concept of a plural society which gains strength through diversity or whether we are to have bitter fragmentation that will result in perpetual tension and strife.—*Earl Warren*

81   Loss of faith in the American proposition is a secret sickness which can bring the country down.—*Archibald MacLeish*

Anarchy

see EXTREMISTS, RADICALS, REVOLUTION, VIOLENCE;
also LAW, ORDER

82   The nineteenth-century British historian Thomas Macaulay wrote to an American friend and predicted the collapse of government in the twentieth century either by dictator or anarchy:
   "Your Constitution is all sail and no anchor."

83   Jeanne Roland, a French leader of the moderate Girondist faction, was condemned to death in 1793 by the radicals, led by Danton. As she was led to the scaffold in a donkey cart, she turned to a statute of liberty and said:

"O liberty, O liberty! What crimes are committed in thy name!"

84   In the Warsaw legislature in the Middle Ages, one legislator could veto an entire act simply by standing up in the chamber in opposition. The guarantee of such individual expression ensures anarchy. The government collapsed.

85   Law is restraint and absence of restraint is anarchy.—*Benjamin Cardozo*

86   There is no grievance that is a fit object for redress by mob law.—*Abraham Lincoln*

87   Order without liberty and liberty without order are equally destructive.—*Theodore Roosevelt*

88   The anarchist plays into the hand of the authoritarian.—*John Gardner*

89   Unlicensed liberty leads necessarily to despotism and anarchism.—*Louis Brandeis*

Apathy

see also INVOLVEMENT

90   The death of democracy is not likely to be an assassination by ambush. It will be a slow extinction from apathy, indifference and undernourishment.—*Robert Maynard Hutchins*

91   Where older generations sought conformity as a substitute for purpose, the new apathy seeks nonconformity as a substitute for ambition.—*Kingman Brewster*

92   The only thing necessary for the triumph of evil is for good men to do nothing.—*Edmund Burke*

93   The hottest places in Hell are reserved for those who in time of great moral crises maintain their neutrality.—*Dante*

94   The worst sin toward our fellow creatures is not to hate them, but to be indifferent to them; that's the essence of inhumanity—*George Bernard Shaw*

95   Tyranny in an oligarchy is less dangerous to the public

welfare than apathy of a citizen in a democracy.—*Baron de Montesquieu*

96   I know thy ways. Thou art neither hot nor cold. Because thou art lukewarm, I shall spew thee out of my mouth.—*Apostle John in* REVELATION

Architecture

see ARTIST, CITY

97   The trouble with our architecture is not its exuberance, but its prima donna complex. It is narcissistic and neurotically antisocial. It refuses to restrain itself in the company of older architecture.—*Wolf von Eckhardt*

98   I call architecture frozen music.—*Goethe*

99   Everything betrays us as a bunch of catch-penny materialists devoted to a blatant insistence on screeching commercialism. —*Edward Durell Stone*

100   Variety of uniformities makes complete beauty.—*Christopher Wren*

101   What we call organic architecture is no mere esthetic nor cult nor fashion, but an actual movement based upon a profound idea of a new integrity of human life, wherein art, religion and science are one: *Form* and *Function* seen as *One,* of such is *Democracy.*—*Frank Lloyd Wright*

102   The age of the machine sounds the death knell for the architect.—*Le Corbusier*

Artist

see CULTURE

103   While going down the St. Lawrence River in 1757 to win Quebec against the French, General Wolfe recited Thomas Gray's "Elegy Written in a Country Churchyard:

> The boast of heraldry, the pomp of pow'r,
> And all that beauty, all that wealth e'er gave,

Awaits alike the inevitable hour:
The paths of glory lead but to the grave.

Then Wolfe, who was to be killed the next day, said: "I'd rather be the poet who wrote those words than the general who took Quebec."

104   In 1805, Napoleon met Goethe at Erfurt. The conqueror said to the poet, "You are a man."

105   Marc Chagall once told his test for art:
"When I judge art, I take my painting and put it next to a God-made object, like a tree or flower. If it clashes, it is not art."

106   Virginia Woolf, wondering in her *Diary* why a certain good novel is not a great book, asks herself what qualities it lacks, and replies:
"That it adds nothing to one's vision of life."

107   Imagination needs a soil in history, tradition, and human institutions, or else random growth is in itself insignificant and like trivial melodies will soon go out of fashion.—*George Santayana*

108   The artist has a special task and duty: the task of reminding men of their humanity and the promise of their creativity.—*Lewis Mumford*

109   A community whose life is not irrigated by art and science, by religion and philosophy, day upon day, is a community that exists half alive.—*Lewis Mumford*

110   Art is the reaching out into the ugliness of the world for vagrant beauty and the imprisoning of it into a tangible dream.—*George Jean Nathan*

111   There are two qualities of art: it is indescribable and inimitable.—*Auguste Renoir*

112   Art is not a pastime, but a priesthood.—*Jean Cocteau*

113   Every time an artist dies, part of the vision of mankind passes with him.—*Franklin D. Roosevelt*

114   All art is a revolt against man's fate.—*André Malraux*

115   Art is like a border of flowers along the course of civilization.—*Lincoln Steffens*

116   A prince must show himself a lover of merit, give prefer-ment to the able, and honor those who excel in every art.—*Nic-colò Machiavelli*

117   Art is a lie that makes us realize the truth.—*Pablo Picasso*

118   Every time I sell a painting of mine, I feel like I'm ampu-tating an arm or leg.—*Pablo Picasso*

119   An armor-plated heart is to a writer what blindness is to an artist or deafness is to a musician.—*Ilya Ehrenburg*

120   Liberty is not an art; liberty must be used to bring some natural art to fruition.—*George Santayana*

121   I must paint humanity, humanity, humanity.—*Vincent Van Gogh*

122   Art is either a revolutionist or a plagiarist.—*Paul Gauguin*

123   Art is a collaboration between God and the artist, and the less the artist the better.—*André Gide*

124   Art flourishes where there is a sense of adventure.—*Alfred North Whitehead*

125   The aim of art is to represent not the outward appearance of things, but their inward significance.—*Aristotle*

126   Every artist is a moralist, though he need not preach.—*George Santayana*

127   We love beauty without extravagance.—*Pericles*

Beginning

see RENEWAL

128   When President John Adams stayed in the White House the first time, the new Executive Mansion, unfinished though it was, was an impressive building. His first night there, he sat down to write Abigail. After telling of his journey from Philadelphia, he added:

"Before I end my letter I pray Heaven to bestow the best of blessings on this house and all that shall hereafter inhabit it. May none but wise and honest men ever rule under this roof."

129   When Benjamin Disraeli was shown the dynamo by its inventor, English scientist Michael Faraday, Prime Minister Disraeli looked at this forerunner of all generators and said, "What good is this?"
Replied Faraday: "What good is a baby, Mr. Disraeli?"

130   After the victory of El Alamein in Africa in 1942, Winston Churchill said in the House of Commons:
"This is not the end. It is not even the beginning of the end. But it is perhaps the end of the beginning."

131   Keep thou my feet, I do not ask to see the distant scene; one step enough for me.—*John Henry Cardinal Newman*

132   The beginning is said to be half the whole.—*Aristotle*

133   There's a new foot on the floor, my friend,
                And a new face at the door, my friend,
                A new face at the door.
                        —*Alfred, Lord Tennyson*

134   A long journey begins with a single step.—*Chinese proverb*

135   The past is but the beginning of a beginning.—*H. G. Wells*

136   Every beginning is a consequence—every beginning *ends* something.—*Paul Valéry*

Brotherhood

see COMPASSION, HUMANITY;
also PREJUDICE

137   Branch Rickey, head of the Brooklyn Dodgers, said to a fellow club owner when he proposed breaking the color line by hiring Jackie Robinson:
"I'm going to make baseball an all-American game."

138   The world has narrowed into a neighborhood before it has broadened into a brotherhood.—*Lyndon B. Johnson*

139   Houses are built of bricks, mortar and goodwill, not politics, prejudices, and spite.—*Winston Churchill*

140   The mystic bond of brotherhood makes all men one.—*Thomas Carlyle*

141   Until you have become really in actual fact a brother of everyone, brotherhood will not come to pass. Only by brotherhood will liberty be saved.—*Fëdor Dostoevski*

142   On this shrunken globe, men can no longer live as strangers. . . . Our prayer is that men everywhere will learn, finally, to live as brothers, to respect each other's differences, to heal each other's wounds, to promote each other's progress, and to benefit from each other's knowledge.—*Adlai Stevenson*

143   To have courage without pugnacity,
        To have conviction without bigotry,
        To have charity without condescension,
        To have faith without credulity,
        To have love of humanity without mere sentimentality,
        To have meekness with power,
        And emotion with sanity,
        That is brotherhood.

                                        —*Charles Evans Hughes*

144   It is easier to love humanity as a whole than to love one's neighbor.—*Eric Hoffer*

145   To correct the evils, great and small, which spring from want of sympathy and from positive enmity among strangers, as nations or as individuals, is one of the highest functions of civilization.—*Abraham Lincoln*

Bureaucracy

see GOVERNMENT, PUBLIC OFFICE

146   Count Leo Tolstoy once described the evils of too much government in this way:
        "I sit on a man's back choking him and making him carry me,

and yet assure myself and others that I am very sorry for him and wish to ease his lot by all possible means—except by getting off his back."

147   I do not rule Russia; ten thousand clerks do.—*Nicholas I*

148   Of all the races in the world our people would be the last to consent to being governed by a bureaucracy.—*Winston Churchill*

149   States, as great engines, move slowly.—*Francis Bacon*

150   The work of internal government has become the task of controlling the thousands of fifth-rate men.—*Henry Adams*

151   Institutional sluggishness thwarts constructive change.—*John Gardner*

152   Bureaucracy is a giant mechanism operated by pygmies.—*Honoré de Balzac*

153   The hallmark of our age is the tension between released aspirations and sluggish institutions.—*John Gardner*

154   It is hard to feel individually responsible with respect to the invisible processes of a huge and distant government.—*John Gardner*

155   We instinctively have greater faith in the counterbalancing effect of many social, philosophical, and economic forces than in arbitrary law. We will not accord to the central government unlimited authority, any more than we will bow our necks to the dictates of the uninhibited seekers after personal power in finance, labor, or any other field.—*Dwight D. Eisenhower*

156   A state which dwarfs its men in order that they may be more docile instruments in its hands even for beneficial purposes—will find that with small men no great thing can really be accomplished.—*John Stuart Mill*

157   But it is not by the consolidation, or concentration, of powers, but by their distribution that good government is effected.—*Thomas Jefferson*

158   Centralization is the death blow of public freedom.—*Benjamin Disraeli*

159   It may be laid as a universal rule that a government which attempts more than it ought will perform less.—*Thomas Macaulay*

Business

160   Few of us can translate the Latin inscription on the back of our dollar bill: *Annuit coeptis*—Be favorable to bold enterprises. Benjamin Franklin chose the seal and the motto for that seal because he knew that new ventures, new enterprises, were the basis for American economy.

161   American capitalism has been both overpraised and over-indicted . . . it is neither the Plumed Knight nor the monstrous Robber Baron.—*Max Lerner*

162   Some see private enterprise as a predatory target to be shot, others as a cow to be milked but few are those who see it as a sturdy horse pulling the wagon.—*Winston Churchill*

163   The business of America is business.—*Calvin Coolidge*

164   In business, the earning of profit is something more than an incident of success. It is an essential condition of success. It is an essential condition of success because the continued absence of profit itself spells failure.—*Louis Brandeis*

165   One must now apologize for any success in business as if it were a violation of the moral law, so that today it is worse to prosper than to be a criminal.—*Isocrates*

166   A great society is a society in which men of business think greatly of their functions.—*Alfred North Whitehead*

167   American business needs a lifting purpose greater than the struggle of materialism.—*Herbert Hoover*

168   Businessmen have protested too much against the caliber of government people, but have done too little about it.—*Lucius Clay*

169   Everyone lives by selling something.—*Robert Louis Stevenson*

170   There are two times in a man's life when he should not speculate: when he can't afford it and when he can.—*Mark Twain*

171   Corporations can no longer stand aside from society's most urgent priorities and expect to satisfy the ambition of young men and women who place idealism ahead of materialism.—*Charles Percy*

172   The capitalist . . . has fulfilled a creative function in history. . . . In free enterprise the spur of competition and the zeal and zest of ownership arouse the productiveness and inventiveness of man.—*Will Durant*

173   Small business is not and never has been a small matter in our national life. Operating or working in small business has not only been a good way to make a living—it has been a good way to help make a country strong and free and prosperous.—*Richard M. Nixon*

174   Every great man of business has got somewhere a touch of the idealist in him.—*Woodrow Wilson*

175   The vice of capitalism is that it stands for the unequal sharing of blessings; whereas the virtue of socialism is that it stands for the equal sharing of misery.—*Winston Churchill*

Challenge

see PROBLEM, RESPONSIBILITY

176   The black activist, the Reverend Jesse Jackson, said at the funeral of his close friend Jackie Robinson: "This man turned a stumbling block into a steppingstone."

177   Now civilizations, I believe, come to birth and proceed to grow by successful responding to successive challenges.—*Arnold Toynbee*

178   As at the Olympic games, it is not the finest and strongest men who are crowned, but they who enter the lists, for out of these

the prize men are selected; so too in life, of the honorable and the good, it is they who act who rightly win the prize.—*Aristotle*

179   Creation is not so easy an enterprise; it wins its ultimate successes through a process of trial and error.—*Arnold Toynbee*

180   I must report that even excellent institutions run by excellent human beings are inherently sluggish, not hungry for innovation, not quick to respond to human need, not eager to reshape themselves to meet the challenge of the times.—*John Gardner*

181   Trouble is only opportunity in work clothes.—*Henry Kaiser*

182   These dark days will be worth all they cost us if they teach us that our true destiny is not to be ministered unto, but to minister to ourselves and to our fellow men.—*Franklin D. Roosevelt*

183   This time, like all other times, is a very good one, if we but know what to do with it.—*Ralph Waldo Emerson*

184   Experience is not what happens to you; it is what you do with what happens to you.—*Aldous Huxley*

Change

see FUTURE, PROGRESS, REFORM;
also REACTIONARY

185   In Lewis Carroll's *Through the Looking-Glass,* the Queen says to Alice:
"It takes all the running you can do to keep in the same place."

186   Alvin Toffler defines "future shock" in his book of that name as "disorientation by premature accelerated change."

187   When arguing against change in the electoral system, Senator John F. Kennedy cited the dictum of Lord Falkland:
"When it is not necessary to change, it is necessary *not* to change."

188   The art of progress is to preserve order amid change and to preserve change amid order.—*Alfred North Whitehead*

189   A state without the means of some change is without the means of its conservation.—*Edmund Burke*

190   When Justice Felix Frankfurter was asked if a man changes when he goes on the Supreme Court, he replied, "If he is any good, he does."

191   Progress is a nice word. But change is its motivator and change has its enemies.—*Robert F. Kennedy*

Citizenship

see CIVIC WORK, GOVERNMENT

192   Nicholas Murray Butler, the President of Columbia University, observed that there were three kinds of people: Those who don't know what's happening; those who do know what's happening; those who make what's happening.

193   Solon, centuries before Christ, wrote into the Athenian constitution the curious provision that all those who avoided taking sides in factional disputes within the commonwealth would be disenfranchised of their citizenship. His harsh provision had a valid basis.

When citizens say that they are above politics, they are saying that democracy is beneath them. They are really dropouts from democracy.

194   The health of a democratic society may be measured by the quality of functions performed by private citizens.—*Alexis de Tocqueville*

195   The true test of civilization is not the census, nor the size of cities, nor the crops—no, but the kind of man the country turns out.—*Ralph Waldo Emerson*

196   The worth of a state, in the long run, is the worth of the individuals composing it.—*John Stuart Mill*

197   A community is like a ship, everyone ought to be prepared to take the helm.—*Henrik Ibsen*

198   It is an old maxim that republics live by virtue—that is by the maintenance of a high level of public spirit.—*Viscount Bryce*

199   Those who expect to reap the benefits of freedom must, like men, undergo the fatigue of supporting it.—*Thomas Paine*

200   Politics is the most important pursuit of man.—*Oswald Spengler*

201   Mere passive good citizenship is not enough. Men and women must be aggressive for what is right, if government is to be saved from those who are aggressive for what is wrong.—*Robert La Follette*

202   As soon as public service ceases to be the chief business of the citizens, and they would rather serve with their money than with their persons, the state is not far from its fall.—*Jean Jacques Rousseau*

203   The first requisite of a good citizen in this republic of ours is that he shall be able and willing to pull his own weight.—*Theodore Roosevelt*

204   The citizen of today is not the voiceless, faceless man of the modern anti-utopias. He can influence government at every level—directly by participation in honest local politics and by choosing men of integrity to represent him at higher levels; indirectly by the views he holds, the courage with which he holds them, the letters he writes to his elected representatives, the lobbies he supports—even with replies he makes to pollsters.—*Barbara Ward*

205   It takes more than leadership to preserve the ideals of a free society. The values we cherish will not survive without the constant attention of the ordinary citizen. Unlike the pyramids, the monuments of the spirit will not stand untended. They must be nourished in each generation by the allegiance of believing men and women.—*John Gardner*

City

see ARCHITECTURE, POVERTY

206   In Saul Bellow's *Adventures of Augie March,* one character asks:
"There haven't been civilizations without cities, but what about cities without civilizations?"

207   Ours is no workaday city. No other provides so many recreations for the spirit—contests and sacrifices all the day long, and beauty in our public buildings to cheer the heart and delight the eyes day by day. . . . We have more at stake than men who have no such inheritance. . . . Let us then draw strength, not merely from the twice-told arguments—how fair and noble a thing it is to show courage in battle—but from the busy spectacle of our great city's life as we have it before us day by day, falling in love with her as we see her, and remembering that all this greatness she owes to men with the fighter's daring, the wise man's understanding of his duty, and the good man's self-discipline in its performance.—*Pericles*

208   The continued dissolution of the city into an amorphous, overmechanized urbanoid mass, lacking both esthetic identity and social character.—*Lewis Mumford*

209   The bureaucratic ideals of standardization, regimentation, and centralized control have left their mark on all our urban planning for the last half century: the city, to paraphrase Aristotle, has become organization man writ large.—*Lewis Mumford*

210   All cities are mad, but the madness is gallant; all cities are beautiful, but the beauty is grim.—*Christopher Morley*

211   Hell is a city much like London.—*Percy Bysshe Shelley*

212   The final mission of the city is to further man's conscious participation in the cosmic and the historic process.—*Lewis Mumford*

213   The government of cities is the one conspicuous failure of the United States.—*Viscount Bryce*

214   In the city time becomes visible.—*Lewis Mumford*

215   Man comes to the city for work, he remains for the good life.—*Aristotle*

216   The men who dwell in the city are my teachers.—*Socrates*

217   New York City is not a melting pot but a boiling pot.— *Thomas Dewey*

218   He who knows the law that will help the city is the true citizen.—*Sophocles*

219   The individual who pollutes the air with his factory and the ghetto kid who breaks store windows both represent the same thing. They don't care about each other—or what they do to each other.—*Daniel Patrick Moynihan*

220   Manufacturers are uniquely capable of severing the infamous suburban "white noose" around the city.—*Jeanne R. Lowe*

221   The serious problems of the cities are largely insoluble now and will be for the foreseeable future.—*Edward Banfield*

222   Only the modern city offers the mind the grounds on which it can achieve awareness of itself.—*Hegel*

223   The city is not obsolete; it's the center of our civilization. —*Edward Logue*

224   You might say of this sprawling megalopolitan nonentity, the anti-city in McLuhan's terminology, that *the mess is the message*. And the more massive the mess the more muddled the message.—*Lewis Mumford*

225   I always seem to suffer from loss of faith on entering cities. —*Ralph Waldo Emerson*

Civic Work

see CITIZENSHIP, RESPONSIBILITY;
also APATHY

226   In his book *Reclaiming the American Dream,* Richard Cornuelle advocates the need for civic action. He writes:

"America has been unique, not because we organize our commercial sector on free enterprise lines or because we elect those who control government, although we talk about these things the most. We have been unique because another sector [the volunteer civic groups] clearly distinct from the other two, has in the past borne a heavy load of public responsibility."

227   I have often admired the extreme skill with which the inhabitants of the United States succeed in proposing a common object for the exertions of a great many men and inducing them voluntarily to pursue it.—*Alexis de Tocqueville*

228   We are going to have to find ways of enlisting all the volunteer talents and resources of our great nation to cope with problems before us. This means not only the mobilization of national, state, and local government; it also means the channeling of investment, capital, modern science, technological skills, business acumen, labor, statesmanship, educational ventures, and intellectual daring.—*Nelson Rockefeller*

Civilization

see CULTURE, PROGRESS;
also DECLINE, MATERIALISM

229   Civilization is progress from an indefinite, incoherent homogeneity toward a definite, coherent heterogeneity.—*Herbert Spencer*

230   This strange disease of modern life with its brisk hurry and divided aims.—*Matthew Arnold*

231   Perfection of means and confusion of goals seem—in my opinion—to characterize our age.—*Albert Einstein*

232   Progress celebrates pyrrhic victories over nature.—*Karl Kraus*

233   Civilization is nothing else but the attempt to reduce force to being the last resort.—*José Ortega y Gasset*

234   The world . . . is only beginning to see that the wealth of a nation consists more than anything else in the number of superior men it harbors.—*William James*

Commitment

see RESOLUTION, SERVICE;
also APATHY

235   Dr. William C. Menninger gave this answer to the question of how to achieve mental health:
   "Find a mission in life and take it seriously."

236   Now while our hearts are open, do not let us close our minds; in our commitments, let us remember the way of performance.—*Learned Hand*

237   It is not knowledge of ways and means we lack, it is the will to put them into effect.—*Alfred Vanderbilt*

238   Man is a kind of creature who cannot be whole except he be committed, because he cannot find himself without finding a center beyond himself. In short, the emancipation of the self requires commitment.—*Reinhold Niebuhr*

Communication

see LEADERSHIP, PUBLIC OPINION, RESPONSIVENESS

239   In the thirteenth century, a *"quod libet"* session in a European university meant that you could ask the professor any questions you wanted.

240   "Ethelred the Unready," was an ineffectual English king in the eleventh century. "Unready" is a poor English translation of the Saxon word "Redeless," which meant "not willing to listen."

241   Although in Western nations shaking your head means "no," in Arab countries it signifies "yes." Nodding your head up and down in Arab nations means "no."

242   It is a luxury to be understood.—*Ralph Waldo Emerson*

243   If the trumpet sounds an uncertain note, who shall prepare for battle?—*Paul in his* SECOND LETTER TO THE CORINTHIANS

Community

see CITIZENSHIP, CITY, CIVIC WORK

244   A great America for which we long is unattainable unless the individuality of the community is far more highly developed and can come through the concentrated strivings of smaller groups. If ideals are developed locally, the national ones will come pretty near taking care of themselves.—*Louis Brandeis*

Compassion

245   Julia Ward Howe once asked Senator Charles Sumner to interest himself in the case of a person who needed some help.

The senator answered, "Julia, I've become so busy I can no longer concern myself with individuals."

Julia replied, "Charles, that is quite remarkable. Even God hasn't reached that stage yet."

246   Lao-tse, the Chinese philosopher in the fifth century, wrote in Tao-Te-king: "Man, when living, is soft and tender; when dead, he is hard and tough. All animals and plants when living are tender and fragile; when dead they become withered and dry. Therefore it is said: 'The hard and tough are parts of death; the soft and tender are parts of life. This is the reason why the soldiers when they are too tough cannot carry the day; the tree when it is too tough will break. The position of the strong and great is low, and the position of the weak and tender is high.' "

247 Compassion is the highest form of human existence.—
Fëdor Dostoevski

248 Perhaps we cannot prevent this world from being a world in which children are tortured, but we can reduce the number of tortured children. If we do not do this, who will?—*Albert Camus*

Compromise

see PRINCIPLES, REALISM, REASON;
also EXTREMISTS

249 Six centuries before Christ, the Greek legislator Solon drafted a new constitution. He was asked by a friend: "Did you give Athens the best laws?"
  Solon replied: "No, the best they could receive."

250 The best is the enemy of the good.—*Voltaire*

251 Manhood begins in a way when we have made a truce with necessity.—*Thomas Carlyle*

252 Of evils we must choose the least.—*Aristotle*

253 There are few things wholly evil or wholly good. Almost everything especially of government policy is an inseparable compound of the two, so that our best judgment of the preponderance between them is continually demanded.—*Abraham Lincoln*

254 Politics is the doctrine of the attainable, the possible.
—*Otto von Bismarck*

255 All legislation . . . is founded upon the principle of mutual confession . . . let him who elevates himself above humanity, above its weaknesses, its infirmities, its wants, say, if he pleases, "I will never compromise," but let no one who is not above human frailties abandon compromise.—*Henry Clay*

256 A rational man acting in the real world may be defined as one who decides where he will strike a balance between what he desires and what can be done.—*Walter Lippmann*

257   Compromise is odious to passionate natures because it seems a surrender; and to intellectual natures because it seems confusion.—*George Santayana*

Conformity

see MEDIOCRITY;
also EXCELLENCE, INDIVIDUAL

258   The cultural and political crisis of our day is not due to the fact that there is too much individualism, but that what we believe to be individualism is an empty shell.—*Erich Fromm*

259   Be not conformed of this world but be transformed by the renewal of your mind.—*Paul in his* LETTER TO THE ROMANS

260   The race of men, while sheep in credulity, are wolves for conformity.—*Carl Van Doren*

261   Whoso would be a man must be a nonconformist.—*Ralph Waldo Emerson*

262   That so few now dare to be eccentric marks the chief danger of the time.—*John Stuart Mill*

263   Integrity simply means a willingness not to violate one's identity.—*Erich Fromm*

Conservatism

see HERITAGE, PATRIOTISM;
also LIBERALISM, REALISM

264   When our first parents were driven out of paradise, Adam is believed to have remarked to Eve: "My dear, we live in an age of transition."—*Dean Inge*

265   The conservative is no utopian; until the end of all things the world is a battleground, a place of testing, and the permanent things will be challenged afresh in every generation.—*T. S. Eliot*

266   Individuals may form a community, but it is institutions alone that create a nation.—*Benjamin Disraeli*

267   What is conservatism? Is it not adherence to the old and tried against the new and untried?—*Abraham Lincoln*

268   To innovate is not to reform.—*Edmund Burke*

269   The only means of conservation is innovation.—*Peter Drucker*

270   Stability is not immobility.—*Prince Metternich*

271   A nation is a work of art, a work wrought of time.— *André Maurois*

272   Put not your ploughshare too deep into new land.—*Sir Walter Scott*

273   The only dependable foundation of personal liberty is the personal economic security of private property; private property was the original source of freedom.—*Walter Lippmann*

274   The most dangerous thing in the world is to leap a chasm in two jumps.—*David Lloyd George*

275   A wise man does not try to hurry history.—*Adlai Stevenson*

Constitution

see CONSERVATISM, GOVERNMENT, LAW;
also ANARCHY, REVOLUTION

276   The Constitution as a whole has stood and stands unshaken. The scales of power have continued to hang fairly even. The President has not corrupted and enslaved Congress. Congress has not paralyzed and cowed the President.—*Viscount Bryce*

277   The Constitution of the United States is not a mere lawyer's document; it is a vehicle of life, and its spirit is always the spirit of the age.—*Woodrow Wilson*

278   Some men look to constitutions with sanctimonious reverence.—*Thomas Jefferson*

279   Is there any political style which is best for all men? I believe there is: constitutional government is best because it best fits the nature of man—the nature of man being an unstable mixture of freedom and fallibility, of selfishness and generosity. Constitutional government seeks to give maximum play to the freedom of the individual while at the same time establishing the necessary restraints and evoking a sense of social cooperation.—*Henry Luce*

Courage

280   In Ernest Hemingway's *The Sun Also Rises,* the lieutenant says:
"It is awfully easy to be hard-boiled about everything in the daytime, but at night it's another thing."

281   Where there is a brave man there is the thickest of the fight, there the post of honor.—*Henry David Thoreau*

282   To be poised against fatality, to meet adverse conditions gracefully, is more than simple endurance; it is an act of aggression, a positive triumph.—*Thomas Mann*

283   A hero is no braver than the ordinary man, but is braver five minutes longer.—*Ralph Waldo Emerson*

284   Nothing requires a rarer intellectual heroism than willingness to see one's equation written out.—*George Santayana*

285   One man with courage makes a majority.—*Andrew Jackson*

286   Courage is that virtue which champions the cause of right. —*Cicero*

287   As to moral courage, I have rarely met with the two o'clock in the morning courage; I mean unprepared courage.—*Napoleon*

288   If there be one thing upon earth that mankind loves and admires more than another it is a brave man—a man who dares

look the devil in the face and tell him he is the devil.—*James A. Garfield*

289   The greatest height of heroism to which an individual, like a people, can attain is to know how to face ridicule.—*Miguel de Unamuno*

290   Behold the turtle. He makes progress only when he sticks his neck out!—*James B. Conant*

Crisis

see CHALLENGE, PROBLEM

291   In 1848, the French philosopher Alexis de Tocqueville feared the effects of the rising turbulence in the French nation. As a deputy in the French Chamber he called upon French political leaders to look into their own hearts. In his closing phrases he said, "In such times as these you are remaining calm before the degradation of public morality. You are speaking of legislative changes and I believe they are necessary. I believe in the need for electoral reform, in the urgency of parliamentary reform . . . but it is not the mechanics of laws that produce great events, gentlemen, but the inner spirit of governments."

292   When written in Chinese, the word "crisis" is composed of two characters—one represents *danger* and one represents *opportunity*.

293   During the darkest days of the Civil War, Abraham Lincoln had the burden to sustain the hopes and goals for the Union. Once when a delegation called at the White House and detailed a catalogue of crises facing America, Lincoln told this story:
"Years ago a young friend and I were out one night when a shower of meteors fell from the clear November sky. The young man was frightened, but I told him to look up in the sky past the shooting stars to the fixed stars beyond shining serene in the firmament, and I said, 'Let us not mind the meteors, but let us keep our eyes on the stars.'"

294   John Witherspoon, the Scottish-born Presbyterian minister, who was President of the College of New Jersey (Princeton) was elected delegate to the Continental Congress in June 1776. Arriving in Philadelphia just in time to hear the debate over independence between John Adams and John Dickinson, he heard the remark, "The Colonies are not yet ripe for a declaration of independence."

He replied: "In my judgment, sir, we are not only ripe, but rotting."

Culture

see ARTIST, CIVILIZATION

295   Culture is the sum of all the forms of art, of love and of thought, which, in the course of centuries, have enabled man to be less enslaved.—*André Malraux*

296   A community whose life is not irrigated by art and science, by religion and philosophy, day upon day, is a community that exists only half alive.—*Lewis Mumford*

297   Culture is on the horns of this dilemma: if profound and noble it must remain rare, if common it must become mean.—*George Santayana*

Decline

see APATHY, MATERIALISM

298   In William Saroyan's play, *The Time of Your Life,* an odd character appears on stage from time to time, muttering to himself, "No foundation—no foundation, all the way down the line."

299   In *The Decline and Fall of the Roman Empire,* Edward Gibbon wrote of "decent easy men, who supinely enjoyed the gifts of the gifts of the founders."

300   In 1940, when a dispirited and complacent France fell to the Nazis, their leader Marshal Pétain sadly wrote:

"Our spirit of enjoyment was greater than our spirit of sacrifice. We wanted to have more than we wanted to give. We spared effort and we met disaster."

301   The enemy is within our own gates; it is with our own luxury, our own folly, our own animality that we have to contend. —*Cicero*

302   If this nation is ever destroyed, it will not be from without, but from within.—*Abraham Lincoln*

303   Though sixteen civilizations have perished already to our knowledge, and nine others may be now at the point of death, we —the twenty-sixth—are not compelled to submit the riddle of fate to the blind arbitrament of statistics. The divine spark of creative power is still alive within us, and if we have the grace to kindle it into flame, then the stars in their courses cannot defeat our efforts to attain the goal of human endeavor.—*Arnold Toynbee*

Example

see EXCELLENCE;
also MEDIOCRITY

304   When Prime Minister William Pitt was toasted in 1805 as the savior of Europe, he accepted with these words:
"I return you many thanks for the honor you have done me. But Europe is not to be saved by any single man. England has saved herself by her exertions and will, I trust, save Europe by her example."

305   The historian Thucydides records Pericles telling the people of Athens: "We do not imitate—but are a model to others."

Excellence

see EXAMPLE, GREATNESS, VOCATION;
also MEDIOCRITY

306   Seventy-seven-year-old Spanish guitarist Andrés Segovia once explained why he still practices the guitar six hours a day:

"When I am asked why I practice so much, I say that it is like the ladder of Jacob. The angels climbed up and down the ladder step by step even though they had wings."

307   A British Embassy official in Washington, getting ready for a visit by Sir Winston Churchill, told the story of an Embassy aide who was once asked about Sir Winston's preferences in food and drink. "Sir Winston's tastes are quite simple," the aide replied. "He is easily pleased with the best of everything."

308   The last words in *Ethics* by the Dutch philosopher Benedict Spinoza are:
"All excellent things.are difficult as they are rare."

309   The Alaskan Eskimos have a word for hard concentration —the word is *garrtsiluni*—patiently working for something to break or burst.

310   Some people may have greatness thrust upon them. Very few have excellence thrust upon them.—*John Gardner*

311   Men do not care how nobly they live, but only how long— although it is within the reach of every man to live nobly but within no man's power to live long.—*Seneca*

312   Each honest calling, each walk of life, has its own elite, its own aristocracy based upon excellence of performance.—*James B. Conant*

313   Democracy is measured not by its leaders doing extraordinary things, but by its citizens doing ordinary things extraordinarily well.—*John Gardner*

314   Ah, but a man's reach should exceed his grasp—or what's a heaven for?—*Robert Browning*

315   To have striven, to have made an effort, to have been true to certain ideals—this alone is worth the struggle. Now and again in a generation one or two snatch something from dull oblivion.—*Sir William Osler*

Expediency

see COMPROMISE, POLITICS

316   Demosthenes, the great Athenian statesman, was asked why the citizenry of Athens failed to rally against the dictatorship of Philip of Macedon in 341 B.C. Demosthenes blamed the leaders for failing to tell the truth to the people: they did not dare to ask the citizenry to make the sacrifices as they had so valiantly in the past.

"If you analyze the problem correctly, you will conclude that the critical problem is chiefly due to those who try to please the citizens rather than tell them what they need to hear."

317   *Tenke* is a Japanese word for moral backsliding—it means compromising your integrity, such as choosing a life not consistent with your ideals.

318   Expediency is the science of exigencies.—*Louis Kossuth*

319   Practical politics consists in ignoring facts.—*Henry Adams*

320   Expediency may tip the scales when arguments are nicely balanced.—*Benjamin Cardozo*

321   It is much safer to keep in step with the parade of opinion than to try to keep up with the swifter movement of events.—*Walter Lippmann*

322   The uplifting élan that is necessary in politics must be something else than the art of the possible.—*Charles de Gaulle*

323   I believe the moral losses of expediency always far outweigh the temporary gains.—*Wendell L. Willkie*

Extremists

see ANARCHY, RADICALS, REVOLUTION

324   Reason without passion is sterile, but passion without reason is hysterical. . . . If we succeed in destroying the discipline of reason, if we make politics a competition in passion, a competition

in emotion, a competition in unreason and violence, the certain outcome will be the defeat of the left.—*Arthur Schlesinger, Jr.*

325 Faith in a holy cause is to a considerable extent a substitute for the lost faith in ourselves.—*Eric Hoffer*

326 No folly is more costly than the folly of intolerant idealism.—*Winston Churchill*

327 Every extreme attitude is a flight from self.—*Eric Hoffer*

328 When passion usurps the name of truth, the very idea of truth is tarnished and defiled.—*George Santayana*

329 A fanatic is one who can't change his mind and won't change the subject.—*Winston Churchill*

Facts

see PROBLEM, TRUTH

330 Gil Blas in Lesage's novel says,
"Facts are stubborn things and before long the very stones will cry aloud against the rascality of these new practitioners."

331 Abraham Lincoln once asked a colleague: "If the tail was called a leg, how many legs would a sheep have?"
The man replied: "Five."
But Lincoln shook his head replying, "To say a sheep has five legs doesn't make it so."

332 In Charles Dickens's *Hard Times,* Mr. Gradgrind announces: "Now what I want is facts. . . . Facts alone are wanted in life."

333 Winston Churchill once described a colleague as "occasionally stumbling over the truth, but always hastily picking himself up and hurrying on as if nothing had happened."

334 We need education in the obvious more than investigation of the obscure.—*Oliver Wendell Holmes*

335 Facts that are not frankly faced have a habit of stabbing us in the back.—*Sir Harold Bowden*

336   Every man has a right to his own opinion. But no man has a right to be wrong in his facts.—*Bernard Baruch*

337   The true test of a liberal mind is a passion for the facts.
—*Oliver Wendell Holmes*

338   Facts are to the mind what food is to the body.—*Edmund Burke*

339   You cannot ask us to take sides against arithmetic. You cannot ask us to take sides against the obvious facts of the situation.—*Winston Churchill*

340   The first step toward improvement is to look the facts in the face.—*Oliver Wendell Holmes*

341   Only by marshaling the facts can we know how to marshal our resources.—*Richard M. Nixon*

342   United wishes and good will cannot overcome brute facts.
—*Winston Churchill*

343   Truth never lost ground by inquiry, because she is most of all reasonable.—*William Penn*

344   To state the facts frankly is not to despair the future nor indict the past.—*John F. Kennedy*

Faith

see PERSEVERANCE, RELIGION, RESOLUTION

345   Eight centuries before Christ, Isaiah told his people: "They that wait upon the Lord shall renew their strength; they shall mount up with wings as eagles; they shall run and not be weary; and they shall walk and not faint."

346   We are free men. We shall remain free, never to be proven guilty of the one capital offense against freedom, a lack of staunch faith.—*Dwight D. Eisenhower*

347   Small wonder that we in this country have a deeply ingrained faith in human regeneration. We believe that given a chance even the degraded and the apparently worthless are capa-

ble of constructive work and great deeds. It is faith founded on experience, not some idealistic theory.—*Eric Hoffer*

348   I know there is a God and that He hates injustice. I see the storm coming and I know His hand is in it, but if He has a place and a part for me, I believe that I am ready.—*Abraham Lincoln*

349   Faith is never identical with piety.—*Karl Barth*

350   Let us then rely on the goodness of our cause and the aid of the Supreme Being, in whose hands victory is, to animate and encourage us to great and noble actions.—*George Washington*

351   Faith is illuminative, not operative; it does not force obedience, though it increases responsibility; it heightens guilt, it does not prevent sin.—*John Henry Cardinal Newman*

Farewell

see GRATITUDE, MEMORIAL, REMEMBRANCE, RETIREMENT

352   When John Bunyan's hero in *Pilgrim's Progress* was summoned across the river of death, he paused on its edge to declare the faith of all first-generation revolutionaries: "My sword I give to him that shall succeed me in my pilgrimage, and my courage and skill to him that can get it. My marks and scars I carry with me to be a witness for me, that I have fought His battles who now will be my Rewarder."

353   John Donne, the seventeenth-century English dean and poet, was about to depart on a diplomatic mission to Germany. In his farewell sermon he said, "Remember me not for my abilities, but remember my labors and my endeavors."

Foreign Policy

see INTERNATIONALISM, PEACE

354   At the end of the War of 1812, Thomas Jefferson wrote Thomas Leiper, a Philadelphia merchant:

"I hope our wisdom will grow with power, and teach us that the less we use our power the greater we will be."

355   Senator Robert F. Kennedy from the fourteenth-floor window in his Manhattan apartment, could see the tugs and barges slicing through the East River. Once, when he saw a boat sailing out, he cried to friends,

"Look at that! There's a ship called *World Justice,* and it is moving away from the United Nations!"

356   While dining with Prime Minister Pitt at 10 Downing Street, Edmund Burke strove to make Pitt understand how critical the national economic situation was. Pitt made light of the danger saying, "This country and this constitution are safe to the day of judgment."

"Yes," replied Burke, "But 'tis the day of no judgment that I am afraid of."

357   Hervé Alphand, the French ambassador to the United States, once met John Foster Dulles, at the beginning of the Suez crisis. And Mr. Dulles said, "Hervé, we are in the middle of a crisis."

And Alphand replied, "Yes, we are in the middle of a crisis. But you are in the middle of a crisis for only two hundred years. We are in the middle of a crisis for fifteen hundred years."

358   The British Prime Minister Lord Stanley once characterized Lord John Russell's foreign policy as "meddle and muddle."

359   Let's face it: in most international differences, elements of right and wrong, comparable to those which prevail in personal relationships are—if they exist at all—simply not discernible to the outsider. . . . Morality then as a channel to individual self-fulfillment—yes, morality in governmental method, as matter of conscience and preference on the part of our people—yes. But morality as a general criterion for measuring and comparing the behavior of different states—no.—*George Kennan*

360   In foreign relations, as in all other relations, a policy has been formed only when commitments and power have been brought into balance.—*Walter Lippmann*

361   Liberty everywhere and anywhere at any price? This is not a rational policy for a nation, even a big one. It is, to speak bluntly, pernicious bombast which, as the applause dies down, can only mislead friend and foe alike. For no nation can or will pay *any* price for liberty *anywhere,* except at the most heroic for its homeland.—*Walter Lippmann*

362   Self-interest is not only a legitimate, but a fundamental cause for national policy: one which needs no cloak of hypocrisy. . . . It is vain to expect governments to act continuously on any other ground than national interest.—*Alfred Thayer Mahan*

Freedom

see LIBERTY;
also REPRESSION

363   In answering a letter from a Westchester farmer, February 5, 1775, Alexander Hamilton wrote: "The sacred rights of mankind are not to be rummaged for among old parchments or musty records. They are written, as with a sunbeam, in the whole volume of human nature, by the hand of the Divinity itself, and can never be erased or obscured by mortal power."

364   In the last sentence of his book on America, Count Alexis de Tocqueville writes: "It depends upon themselves whether the principle of equality is to lead them to servitude or freedom, to knowledge or barbarism, to prosperity or wretchedness."

365   Freedom is participation in power.—*Cicero*

366   Freedom—no word was ever spoken that has held out greater hope, demanded greater sacrifice, needed more to be nurtured, blessed more the giver, damned more the destroyer or come closer to being God's will on earth. May America ever be its protector.—*Omar Bradley*

367   There is a higher concept of freedom than something that can be conferred or withdrawn, something that is an accident of birth. Freedom is an endowment of every human soul.—*Peter Marshall*

368   A free society is one where it is safe to be unpopular.—*Adlai Stevenson*

369   No one ever heard of state freedom, much less did anyone ever hear of state morals. Freedom and morals are the exclusive possession of individuals.—*Henry Wriston*

370   Rights are not what government must do for us—rights are what our government cannot do for us. Rights are not guarantees by the government—rights are guarantees against the government—even against our own government—because we want to keep it a good government.—*Harold Dodd*

371   We have confused the free with the free and easy.—*Adlai Stevenson*

372   Freedom only exists when the citizens take care of their government.—*Woodrow Wilson*

373   Freedom is not an ideal, it is not even a protection if it means nothing more than the freedom to stagnate.—*Adlai Stevenson*

374   The essence of freedom is the practicability of purpose.—*Alfred North Whitehead*

375   Freedom imposes a burden.—*Learned Hand*

376   A man should never put on his best trousers when he goes out to battle for freedom and truth.—*Henrik Ibsen*

377   Freedom is a good horse, but you must ride it somewhere.—*Matthew Arnold*

378   The cause of freedom is the cause of God.—*Edmund Burke*

379   We think we are emancipated but we are just unbuttoned.—*T. S. Eliot*

380   When the freedom they wished for most was freedom from responsibility, then Athens ceased to be free and never was free again.—*Edith Hamilton*

381   Western freedom will not survive just because it is a whole ideal . . . it will survive . . . if we take freedom down with us into the hurly-burly of competition and conflict and prove that a free society can make itself the good society.—*Walter Lippmann*

382   If a nation values anything more than freedom, it will lose its freedom; and the irony of it is that if it is comfort or money that it values more, it will lose that too.—*Somerset Maugham*

383   The winning of freedom is not to be compared to the winning of a game—with the victory recorded forever in history. Freedom has its life in the hearts, the actions, the sports of men and in it must be daily earned and refreshed—else like a flower cut from its life-giving roots, it will wither and die.—*Dwight D. Eisenhower*

Future

see CHANGE, REFORM, RENEWAL, VISION;
also HISTORY

384   In Paris, there is a statue to the famous French reformer and statesman, Léon Gambetta. On the base is inscribed a sentence of his which epitomizes his career: "No man can forbid us the future."

385   Every human being is a Janus—we look before and after. —*Arnold Toynbee*

386   Real generosity toward the future consists in giving all to what is present.—*Albert Camus*

387   I hold that man is in the right who is most closely in league with the future.—*Henrik Ibsen*

388   Life is a series of collisions with the future; it is not a sum of what we have been but what we yearn to be.—*José Ortega y Gasset*

389   It is the business of the future to be dangerous.—*Alfred North Whitehead*

Government

see POWER, PUBLIC OFFICIALS;
also BUREAUCRACY

390   "Machinery of government" has become a banality. Over the years, the gears-and-levers figure of speech took on a truth of its own, as if a mesh in Washington were the process of government. President William Howard Taft listened in wonderment to an adviser who briefed him on "the machinery of government" and said later to a friend: "You know—he really thinks it *is* machinery."

391   The art of government is not to let men grow stale.—*Napoleon*

392   The art of government is the organization of idolatry.—*George Bernard Shaw*

393   Governments, like clocks, go from the motion men give them, and as governments are made and moved by them, so by them are they ruined too. Therefore, governments rather depend on men than men upon governments.—*William Penn*

394   Consider in fact a body of 658 miscellaneous persons, set to consult about business, with twenty-seven millions, mostly fools, assiduously listening to them, and checking and criticizing them. Was there ever, since the world began, will there ever be till the world ends, any "business" accomplished in these circumstances? —*Thomas Carlyle*

395   Government after all is a very simple thing.—*Warren G. Harding*

396   For in reason, all government without the consent of the governed is the very definition of slavery.—*Jonathan Swift*

397   Government is a contrivance of human wisdom to provide for human wants.—*Edmund Burke*

398   There is no right government except good government. —*George Santayana*

399   A government is free in proportion to the rights it guarantees to the minority.—*Alfred Landon*

400   All free governments, whatever their name, are in reality governments by public opinion and it is on this quality of public opinion that their prosperity depends.—*James Russell Lowell*

401   Government is not a machine but a living thing, modified to its environment . . . shaped to its functions by the sheer pressure of life.—*Woodrow Wilson*

402   A government is not made representative or just by the mechanical expedient of electing its members by universal suffrage. It becomes representative only by embodying in its policy, whether by instinct or high intelligence, the people's conscious and unconscious interests.—*George Santayana*

403   The state has become indeed a "mortal god" and for an age that believes no longer in an immortal god, the state becomes the only god there is.—*Hans Morgenthau*

404   The necessary and constructive use of government must not lead to a doctrinaire and expedient use of government.—*Dwight D. Eisenhower*

Gratitude

see MEMORIAL, REMEMBRANCE

405   Isaac Newton, discoverer of the law of gravity, acknowledged his debt to Descartes and other scientists:
    "If I have seen further, it was by standing upon the shoulders of giants."

Greatness

see EXCELLENCE, LEADERSHIP;
also MEDIOCRITY

406   In Shakespeare's *Twelfth Night,* the character Malvolio receives a note that reads:

Be not afraid of greatness;
Some are born great, some achieve greatness
And some have greatness thrust upon 'em.

407   A static hero is a public liability. Progress grows out of motion.—*Richard E. Byrd*

408   The best claim that a college education can possibly make in your respect, the best thing it can aspire to accomplish for you is this: that it should help you to know a good man when you see him.—*William James*

409   Great is he who uses earthenware as if it were silver; no less great is he who uses silver as if it were earthenware.—*Seneca*

410   A great man is made up of qualities that meet or make great occasions.—*James Russell Lowell*

411   Great men are guideposts and landmarks in the state. —*Edmund Burke*

412   Our slow world spends its time catching up with the ideas of its best minds. It would seem that in almost every generation men are born who embody the projected consciousness of their time and people.—*Woodrow Wilson*

413   Greatness lies not in being strong, but in the right use of strength.—*Henry Ward Beecher*

414   One must wait until the evening to see how splendid the day was.—*Sophocles*

415   Greatness consists not in the holding of some future office, but really consists in doing great deeds with little means and the accomplishment of vast purposes from the private ranks of life. —*Russell Conwell*

416   History is made by men who have the restlessness, impressionability, credulity, capacity for make-believe, ruthlessness and self-righteousness of children. It is made by men who set their hearts on toys. All leaders strive to turn their followers into children.—*Eric Hoffer*

417   Greatness is spontaneous.—*George Santayana*

418   If any man seeks greatness, let him forget greatness and seek truth, and he shall find both.—*Horace Mann*

Heritage

see HISTORY, PATRIOTISM

419   In his Letter to the Hebrews (a Judeo-Christian community in Rome) the writer identified as Apollos of Alexandria in Egypt tells the colony threatened by the persecution of Nero to stand up for their ancestors and to remember their heritage.

420   When the British Queen Mother Elizabeth attended a Williamsburg dedication ceremony in 1957, she said at Bruton Parish Church as she was ushered in, "I want to sit in George Washington's seat."

421   Once Count Sforza met in New York State an Italian-American by the name of Matthews who said he changed his name from Mazzei. Sforza reprimanded him for giving up the heritage of his great name. Count Sforza reminded him that Philip Mazzei was the mentor and friend of Thomas Jefferson.

422   When the Armada was threatening England Queen Elizabeth said, "I know I have the body of a weak and feeble woman, but I have the heart and stomach of a king, and a king of England, too."

423   Carl Sandburg said, when Congress invited him to address the Joint Session in 1965, "If I added to their pride of America, I am happy."

424   On the National Archives Building in Washington is engraved this inscription:
    "The heritage of the past is the seed that brings forth the harvest of the future."

425   Our American heritage is threatened as much by our own indifference as by the most unscrupulous office or by the most powerful foreign threat.—*Dwight D. Eisenhower*

426   A splendid storehouse of integrity and freedom has been bequeathed to us by our forefathers. In this day of confusion, of peril to liberty, our high duty is to see that this storehouse is not robbed of its contents.—*Herbert Hoover*

427   If a man is fortunate he will, before he dies, gather up as much as he can of his civilized heritage and transmit it to his children.—*Will Durant*

428   Patriotism is praiseworthy competition with one's ancestors.—*Tacitus*

429   People will not look forward to posterity who never look backward to their ancestors.—*Edmund Burke*

430   It is indeed a desirable thing to be well descended, but the glory belongs to our ancestors.—*Plutarch*

431   To each generation comes its patriotic duty; and that upon your willingness to sacrifice and endure as those before you have sacrificed and endured rests the national hope.—*Charles Evans Hughes*

432   The debts we owe our ancestors we should repay by handing down entire those sacred rights to which we ourselves were born.—*George Mason*

433   People who take no pride in the noble achievement of remote ancestors will never achieve anything worthy to be remembered with pride by remote descendants.—*Thomas Macaulay*

434   That which thy ancestors have bequeathed, earn it again if thou wouldst possess it.—*Goethe*

History

see HERITAGE;
also FUTURE

435   In front of the Archives Building in Washington, D.C., there is a statue inscribed with a phrase from Shakespeare's *Tempest:*
    "What is past is prologue."

436   Whittaker Chambers wrote to William Buckley in one of his last letters: "History hit us with a freight train."

437   When to the sessions of sweet silent thought
             I summon up remembrance of things past.
                                        —*William Shakespeare*

438   There is no Past that we can bring back to us by the longing for it, there is only the eternally new Now that builds and creates itself out of the elements of the Past as the Past withdraws. The true desire to bring the Past back to us must always be productive.—*Goethe*

439   Like watermen, who look astern while they row the boat ahead.—*Plutarch*

440   The men who make history have no time to write about it. —*Prince Metternich*

441   The mission of the historian is discovery. We should try to grasp the entire experience of a people in the past.—*Daniel Boorstin*

442   History unfolds itself by strange and unpredictable paths. We have little control over the future, and none at all over the past.—*Winston Churchill*

443   He who is ignorant of what happened before his birth is always a child.—*Cicero*

444   I know of no way of judging the future save by the past. —*Patrick Henry*

445   The principal office of history I take to be this: to prevent virtuous actions from being forgotten.—*Tacitus*

446   History and painting are similar. Sir Joshua Reynolds said he mixed his brains with paint. So Macaulay and Parkman mixed their ink with brains. A photographic flat representation of Wolfe at Quebec may be the superficial truth, but it lacks the inner truth. —*Allan Nevins*

447   We cannot say "the past is past" without surrendering the future.—*Winston Churchill*

448 History is past politics and politics present history.—*Woodrow Wilson*

449 Life must be lived forwards, but can only be understood backwards.—*Søren Kierkegaard*

450 A page of history is worth a volume of logic.—*Oliver Wendell Holmes*

451 History is simply a piece of paper covered with print; the main thing is still to make history, not to write it.—*Otto von Bismarck*

452 All history is an inarticulate Bible.—*Thomas Carlyle*

453 Historic continuity with the past is not a duty, it is only a necessity.—*Oliver Wendell Holmes*

454 Let us not be a generation recorded in future histories as destroying the irreplaceable inheritance of life formed through eons past.—*Charles Lindbergh*

455 History is a nightmare from which I am trying to awake. —*James Joyce*

Humanity

see BROTHERHOOD, CIVILIZATION, COMPASSION, WELFARE

456 In the preface of *Look Homeward Angel,* Thomas Wolfe wrote:

> Which of us has known his brother?
> Which of us has looked into his father's heart?
> Which of us is not forever prison-pent?
> Which of us is not forever a stranger and alone?

457 Suetonius in *Lives of the Twelve Caesars* tells how the Emperor Titus said at supper: "Friends—I have lost a day." He was reflecting how he had helped no one that day.

458 About 1140, Peter, Abbot of Cluny, wrote to a Father Bernard these following few and devastating words: "You perform all the difficult religious duties: you fast, you watch, you suffer; but you will not endure the easy ones: you do not love."

459   When Grandma Moses was asked at ninety-three what she was proudest of, she replied, "I've helped some people."

460   The prophet Isaiah in 720 B.C., during the reign of King Hezekiah, denounced Judah and Jerusalem for social injustice. He admonished: "Learn to do well; seek judgment, relieve the oppressed, judge the fatherless, plead for the widow."

461   About a month before Robert F. Kennedy was killed, the British television personality David Frost taped an interview with him. Toward the end of the interview, Frost asked him, "How would you like to be remembered? What would you like the first line of your obituary to say?"

Kennedy's reply was: "Something about the fact that I made some contribution to either my country, or those who were less well off. I think again back to what Camus wrote about the fact that perhaps this world is a world in which children suffer, but we can lessen the number of suffering children, and if you do not do this, then who will do this? I'd like to feel that I'd done something to lessen that suffering."

462   William Faulkner, in his acceptance of the Nobel Prize for Literature, said, "I decline to accept the end of man. . . . I believe that man will not merely endure: he will prevail. He is immortal not because he alone among creatures has an unexhaustible voice, but because he has a soul, a spirit capable of compassion and sacrifice and endurance."

463   Why should there not be a patient hope in the ultimate justice of the people? Is there any better or equal hope in the world?—*Abraham Lincoln*

464   Humanitarianism . . . consists in never sacrificing a human being to a purpose.—*Albert Schweitzer*

465   Men of integrity, by their very existence, rekindle the belief that as a people we can live above the level of moral squalor. —*John Gardner*

466   Each of us has to work out his salvation in his own way. The most that another can do is to be able to give a helping hand. —*Oliver Wendell Holmes*

467   I have labored carefully not to mock, lament and execrate the actions of men; I have labored to understand them.—*Benedict Spinoza*

468   Treat people as if they were what they ought to be and you help them to become what they are capable of being.—*Goethe*

469   A man does not live for himself alone. He lives also for all men on earth.—*Martin Luther*

470   We may go to the moon but that is not very far. The greatest distance we have to cover still lies within ourselves.—*Charles de Gaulle*

471   The spirit's foe in man has not been simplicity but his sophistication.—*George Santayana*

472   Man is designed to be a comprehensivist.—*Buckminster Fuller*

473   A man becomes truly Man only when in quest of what is most exalted in him.—*André Malraux*

474   The ancient world, we may remind ourselves, was not destroyed because the traditions were false. They were submerged, neglected, lost.—*Walter Lippmann*

475   Equality of opportunity, the worth and dignity of the individual brotherhood, individual responsibility, justice, liberty. These are the values . . . of the Western World. The task is to make them live in our institutions.—*John Gardner*

476   What kind of human being are we trying to produce? Not the power man, not the profit man, nor the mechanics man, but the whole man must be the central actor in the new civilization.—*Lewis Mumford*

Idealism

see COMMITMENT, PRINCIPLES, YOUTH, ZEAL

477   Elihu Root said about Charles Evans Hughes in 1925: "He subdued his idealism to the uses of mankind."

478   Thomas Carlyle's bookplate was a picture of a candle and the words "I burn that I may be of use."

479   Justice Oliver Wendell Holmes once wrote to his English law friend Pollock, "You and I believe that high-mindedness is not impossible to man."

480   Senator Robert F. Kennedy said shortly before he was assassinated, "Each time a man stands up for an ideal or sets to improve the lot of others, or strikes out against injustices, he sends forth a ripple of hope."

481   When Carl Schurz told Ralph Waldo Emerson that he thought his Fourth of July speech in Boston had too many "glittering generalities," Emerson replied, "They are not glittering generalities; they are blazing ubiquities."

482   The French writer Jean de Crèvecoeur in *Letters from an American Farmer* wrote during our Revolution: "The American is a new man who acts upon his principles."

483   We are not steering by forms of government, we are steering by principles of government.—*Woodrow Wilson*

484   We are capable at the same time of taking risks and of estimating them beforehand. Others are brave out of ignorance. When they stop to think, they begin to fear. But the man who can be most truly accounted brave is he who best knows the meaning of what is sweet in life and of what is terrible, then goes out to meet what is to come.—*Pericles*

485   Ideals are like stars. You will not succeed in touching them with your hands, but the seafaring man who follows the waters, follows the stars, and if you choose them as your guide, you can reach your destiny.—*Carl Schurz*

486   But he who is a partisan of principle is a prince of citizenship.—*Albert Beveridge*

487   Idealism is the noble toga that political gentlemen drape over their will to power.—*Aldous Huxley*

Ideas

see VISION

488 The next century's task will be to rediscover its gods. —*André Malraux*

489 One of the greatest pains to human nature is the pain of a new idea.—*Walter Bagehot*

490 It is useless to close the gates against ideas; they overleap them.—*Prince Metternich*

491 Daring ideas are like chessmen moved forward; they may be beaten, but they may start a winning game.—*Goethe*

492 Most men think dramatically, not quantitatively.—*Oliver Wendell Holmes*

493 Taking a new step, uttering a new word is what people fear most.—*Fëdor Dostoevski*

494 Yesterday's idea does not influence that of today. It influences a man who reacts with a new idea.—*José Ortega y Gasset*

495 Revolutions do not occur because new ideas suddenly develop, but because a new generation begins to take old ideas seriously.—*Kenneth Keniston*

496 Every now and then a man's mind is stretched by a new idea and never shrinks back to its former dimensions.—*Oliver Wendell Holmes*

497 The vitality of thought is in adventure. Ideas won't keep. Something must be done about them. When the idea is new, its custodians have fervor, live for it, and, if need be, die for it.—*Alfred North Whitehead*

Individual

see ADVENTURE;
also CONFORMITY

498 When Adlai Stevenson was being driven to the airport one day and introduced himself, he started passing the time of day with the cabbie.

"People say I talk over the head of the average man," Stevenson said. "What do you think?"

The cabdriver pondered the question. Then, "Well, Governor, I understand you, but I'm not so sure about the average man."

499   "You are all absurd," Prince Myshkin says to the other characters in Dostoevski's *The Idiot.* "Therefore you are promising material."

500   Man is not the creature of circumstances; circumstances are the creatures of men.—*Benjamin Disraeli*

501   Every individual has a place to fill in the world and is important in some respect whether he chooses to be so or not.— *Nathaniel Hawthorne*

502   The four cornerstones of character on which the structure of this nation was built are: initiative, imagination, individuality and independence.—*Eddie Rickenbacker*

503   If he cannot be assigned to a category, if he is not a model of something, a half of what is needed is there. He is still free from himself, he has acquired an atom of immortality.—*Boris Pasternak*

504   The infantile cowardice of our time which demands an external pattern, a non-human authority.—*Archibald MacLeish*

505   The image-managers encourage the individual to fashion himself into a smooth coin, negotiable in any market.—*John Gardner*

506   I sing of the infinitude of the private man.—*Ralph Waldo Emerson*

507   I think we should be men first and subjects afterward.— *Henry David Thoreau*

Inflation

see SPENDING, TAXATION

508   Marco Polo told how in ancient China the emperors began to issue paper money. One of the ministers got a great revenue by

this scheme. But it soon came about that you could scarcely buy a bowl of rice for ten thousand bills.

509   Far from being a new malaise, inflation is almost as old as man's written records. The Babylonian Code of Hammurabi (c. 2000 B.C.), which was the world's first known detailed system of law, contained regulations on payments and measures for grain and other products that added up to a form of price control.

510   A disordered currency is one of the greatest political evils. —Daniel Webster

511   We cannot protect the dollar by passing the buck.—Richard M. Nixon

512   Inflation is the most important fact of our time, the single greatest peril to our economic health.—Bernard Baruch

513   When national debts have once been accumulated to a certain degree, there is scarce, I believe, a single instance of their having been fairly and completely paid. The liberation of the public revenue, if it has been brought about at all, has always been brought about by a bankruptcy.—Adam Smith

514   Living in an economy with an unstable currency is like living in a society in which no one tells the truth. The ability of modern governments to keep their money straight is an essential condition of their ability to govern.—Gabriel Hauge

515   In the economic arena, only two sections of the people— organized labor and organized capital—are free even in truth. The individual is not free even within these two powerful camps, and the large section of the people that is not entrenched in either camp is being ground down by the inflation for which this kind of freedom keeps the door wide open.—Arnold Toynbee

516   The first panacea for a mismanaged nation is inflation of the currency; the second is war. Both bring a temporary prosperity; both bring a permanent ruin. Both are the refuge of political and economic opportunists.—Ernest Hemingway

Institutions

see BUREAUCRACY, CHANGE, RESPONSIVENESS

517   Reputation and tradition are effective cosmetics for the fading institution.—*John Gardner*

518   All of our institutions must now turn their full intention to the great task ahead—to humanize our lives and thus to humanize our society.—*James Perkins*

519   In institutions the corroding effect of routine can be withstood only by maintaining high ideals of work; but these become the sounding brass and tinkling cymbals without corresponding sound practice.—*Sir William Osler*

520   Most human organizations that fall short of their goals do so not because of stupidity or faulty doctrines, but because of internal decay and rigidification. They grow stiff in the joints. They get in a rut. They go to seed.—*John Gardner*

Intellectual

see REASON, SCHOLAR

521   Every man who expresses an honest thought is a soldier in the army of intellectual liberty.—*Robert Ingersoll*

522   I suspect that a neurotic sense of tidiness in political arrangements can be a great danger to any society.—*George F. Kennan*

523   To the intellectual, the struggle for freedom is more vital than the actuality of a free society. He would rather work, fight, talk for liberty than have it.—*Eric Hoffer*

524   Intellectual blemishes, like facial ones, grow more prominent with age—*La Rochefoucauld*

525   The scholar must be brave and free.—*Ralph Waldo Emerson*

526   Intellectual anarchy is full of lights; its blindness is made up of dazzling survivals, revivals and fresh beginnings.—*George Santayana*

527   An intellectual is a man who takes more words than necessary to tell what he knows.—*Dwight D. Eisenhower*

528   Intellectuals cannot tolerate the chance event, the unintelligible; they have a nostalgia for the absolute, for a universally comprehensive scheme.—*Raymond Aron*

529   The virtue of liberalism is a sort of intellectual kindness or courtesy to all possible wills.—*George Santayana*

Internationalism

see FOREIGN POLICY, PEACE, WAR

530   President John F. Kennedy once quoted Alexander Hamilton's remark at the founding of our country, "We must learn to think continentally." Then Kennedy said, "Today we must learn to think inter-continentally."

531   When the astronaut James Lovell received the Presidential Medal of Freedom, he spoke of the loneliness and sterility of space. He remembered seeing our planet in the distance with its color of life, he said, and he realized that "Earth was the only place we had to go."

532   We are citizens of the world; and the tragedy of our times is that we do not know this.—*Woodrow Wilson*

533   The white race is in the minority, the free enterprise system is in the minority and the majority are looking at us harder and longer than they ever looked before.—*John F. Kennedy*

534   This organization (the U.N.) is created to prevent you from going to hell; it isn't created to take you to heaven.—*Henry Cabot Lodge*

535   What we lawyers want to do is to substitute courts for carnage, dockets for rockets, briefs for bombs, warrants for warheads, mandates for missiles.—*Charles Rhyne*

536 There is a show . . . called *Stop the World, I Want to Get Off*—we do not choose to exercise that option.—*John F. Kennedy*

537 On the international scene, the individual nation is by far the strongest moral force, and the limitations which a supranational morality is able to impose today upon international politics are both fewer and weaker than at almost any time since the end of the Thirty Years' War.—*Hans Morgenthau*

538 Democracy, with its promise of international peace, has been no better guarantee against war than the old dynastic rule of kings.—*Jan C. Smuts*

539 We prefer world law in the age of self-determination—we reject world war in the age of mass extermination.—*John F. Kennedy*

540 Human sovereignty transcends national sovereignty.— *Lester Pearson*

541 We must thread our way between imperialism and isolationism, between the disavowal of the responsibilities of our power and the assertion of our power beyond our resources.—*Adlai Stevenson*

542 The world at our mid-century is like a drum—strike it anywhere and it resounds everywhere.—*Adlai Stevenson*

Involvement

see ACTION, ADVENTURE, CIVIC WORK;
also APATHY

543 Winston Churchill sent to the British ambassador to Greece, during the events of 1944, a stinging reply when the latter complained that he felt as if he were sitting on the top of a volcano: "Where in the hell," went Churchill's cable, "do you expect to be sitting in times like these?"

544 Ralph Waldo Emerson once called at the Concord jail to see his friend, Henry Thoreau, sentenced for refusing to pay taxes to a town that indirectly supported the Mexican War. The author of *Self-Reliance* was puzzled by the situation.

"Henry," he said, "Why are you here?"

"Waldo, why are you *not* here?" was the curt reply.

545   When Goethe was dying, one of his followers asked if he would leave to the world the solution of its many problems and Goethe replied: "If every man would keep his own doorstep clean, very soon the whole world would be clean."

546   When the Duke of Wellington sat for a statue, the sculptor tried to get him to look warlike. All his efforts were in vain, for Wellington seemed too passive.

The sculptor said, "Can you not tell me what you were doing before, say, the Battle of Salamanca? Were you not galloping about the fields, cheering your men to action?"

"No," said the duke scornfully. "If you really want to model me as I was on the morning of Salamanca, then do me crawling along a ditch on my stomach with a telescope in my hand."

547   In Shakespeare's *Henry V,* King Henry says before the battle:

And gentlemen in England, now abed,
Shall think themselves accursed they are not here,
And hold their manhoods cheap, whiles any speaks
That fought with us upon Saint Crispin's day.

548   We cannot safely leave politics to the politicians.—*Henry George*

549   As soon as the public business ceases to be the chief business of the citizen, the nation will fall.—*John Adams*

Justice

see LAW, ORDER

550   More than 2,500 years ago in Judea, a prophet named Micah asked: "What does the Lord require of thee but to do justice, to love mercy and to walk humbly with thy God?"

551   Finley Peter Dunne has his Irish bartender Mr. Dooley

say: "Justice is blind. Blind she is, an' deef an' dumb an' has a wooden leg."

552   Justice and power must be brought together so that whatever is just may be powerful and whatever is powerful may be just. —*Blaise Pascal*

553   The administration of justice is the firmest pillar of government.—*George Washington*

554   Man's capacity for good makes democracy possible but man's inclination to evil makes justice necessary.—*Reinhold Niebuhr*

555   Justice is truth in action.—*Benjamin Disraeli*

556   Justice delayed is justice denied.—*William E. Gladstone*

557   Fairness is what justice really is.—*Potter Stewart*

558   If we are to keep democracy, there must be one commandment: "Thou shalt not ration justice."—*Learned Hand*

559   I think the first duty of society is justice.—*Alexander Hamilton*

560   Justice, though due to the accused, is due to the accuser too.—*Benjamin Cardozo*

561   Nothing alarms America so much as rifts, divisions, the drifting apart of elements among her people, and the thing we ought all to strive for is to close up every rift; and the only way to do it . . . is to establish justice—justice with a heart in it, justice with a pulse in it, justice with sympathy in it.—*Woodrow Wilson*

562   Justice is everybody's business. . . . It affects every man's fireside; it passes on his property, his reputation, his liberty, his life.—*Tom Clark*

563   Tumult arises when justice is dragged away.—*Hesiod*

564   Justice is the earnest and constant will to render to every man his due. The precepts of the law are these: to live honorably, to injure no other man.—*Justinian I*

565   Justice is an ideal which exists in the hearts as well as the minds of men.—*Learned Hand*

566   Judging from the main portions of the history of the world so far, justice is always in jeopardy.—*Walt Whitman*

567   In the public administration of justice mercy to one may be cruelty to others.—*Joseph Addison*

568   Shakespeare's King Lear, blind to his own abuse of power when he was himself king, sees clearly in his outcast role the relativity of justice:

> "See how yond justice rails upon yond simple thief,
>   Hark in thine ear. Change places, and handy-dandy,
>   Which is the justice, which is the thief?"

Knowledge

see REASON

569   It is . . . of no purpose to discuss the use of knowledge—man wants to know, and when he ceases to do so he is no longer man.—*Fridjtof Nansen*

570   Odin was a Norse god who was willing to give up one eye in exchange for knowledge.
     So many students are willing to give up their judgment and impartiality in the pursuit of what they think is "intellectual" or the right thing to believe.

571   Franklin D. Roosevelt, a few days after his inauguration in 1933, called on ninety-two-year-old Justice Oliver Wendell Holmes. He found Holmes in his library, reading Plato. The question rose irresistibly. "Why do you read Plato, Mr. Justice?"
     "To improve my mind, Mr. President," Holmes replied.

572   Knowledge is more than equivalent to force.—*Samuel Johnson*

573   Ignorance is not innocence, but sin.—*Robert Browning*

Law

see JUSTICE, ORDER;
also ANARCHY

574   In a court-trial drama written by Judge Curtis Bok, the plaintiff, who happened to be a sculptor, at one point asked the judge in frustration, "Isn't this a court of justice?"

"No," replied the judge, "it is a court of law. Justice is an ideal like truth or beauty. As you try to achieve beauty with your mallet and chisel—so law is our tool in the pursuit of justice."

575   In Shakespeare's *Measure for Measure,* Angelo, the Lord Deputy of Vienna, warns:

> We must not make a scarecrow of the law,
> Setting it up to fear the birds of prey,
> And let it keep one shape, till custom make it
> Their perch and not their terror.

576   Shakespeare in *Henry VI* dramatizes in Jack Cade's attempted revolution the popular distrust against lawyers. Dick (the butcher) says to Cade, "The first thing we do, let's kill all the lawyers."

And Cade replies, "Nay, that I mean to do."

577   Justice is the insurance we have on our lives and property; obedience is the premium we pay for it.—*William Penn*

578   The end of law is not to abolish and restrain freedom, but to preserve and enlarge freedom.—*John Locke*

579   Scarcely any political question arises in the United States which is not resolved sooner or later into a judicial question.—*Alexis de Tocqueville*

580   Law is the last result of human wisdom acting upon human experience for the benefit of the public.—*Samuel Johnson*

581   Litigious terms, fat contentions and flowing fees.—*John Milton*

582   If the dignity of the law is not sustained, its sun is set never to be lighted up again.—*Thomas Erskine*

583   Not all the heroic victims of legality are martyrs to a noble cause.—*George Santayana*

584   Life and law must be kept closely in touch, as you can't adjust life to law, you must adjust law to life. The only point in having law is to make life work. Otherwise, there will be explosions.—*Arnold Toynbee*

585   Not of the letter but of the spirit, for the letter killeth but the spirit giveth life.—*Paul in his* SECOND LETTER TO THE CORINTHIANS

586   The people should fight for the law as for their city wall. —*Heraclitus*

587   No man is above the law and no man is below it.—*Theodore Roosevelt*

588   In reality the man who defies or flouts the law is like the proverbial fool who saws away the plank on which he sits, and disrespect or disregard for law is the most fundamental of all social virtues, for the alternative to the rule of law is that of violence and anarchy.—*Sir Arthur Bryant*

589   The laws of a nation form the most instructive portion of its history.—*Edward Gibbon*

590   Law is nothing unless close behind it stands a warm living public opinion.—*Wendell Phillips*

591   A lawyer with history or literature is a mechanic, a mere working mason; if he possess some knowledge of these he may venture to call himself an architect.—*Sir Walter Scott*

592   I cannot believe that a republic could hope to exist at the present time if the influence of lawyers in public business did not increase in proportion to the power of people.—*Alexis de Tocqueville*

593   The rational study of law is still to a large extent the study of history.—*Oliver Wendell Holmes*

594   Of all the tasks of government the most basic is to protect its citizens against violence.—*John Foster Dulles*

Leadership

see GOVERNMENT, PUBLIC OFFICE, PUBLIC OPINION;
also MEDIOCRITY

595   The Caliph Haroun-al Raschid used to disguise himself and walk about the city at night to hear what his people were saying.

596   Former President Charles de Gaulle nicknamed his favorite cheese "Pompidou" after his prime minister because "it is soft on the outside, and firm inside."

597   When Abraham Lincoln received a dispatch from his general, Joe Hooker, entitled "Headquarters in the Saddle," Lincoln commented, "The trouble with Hooker is he's got his headquarters where his hindquarters ought to be."

598   "Toom Tabard" (The Empty Cloak) was the nickname of John de Baliol, the impotent and ineffectual king of Scotland in the thirteenth century. The Scottish people felt that the reign of de Baliol was like having no king at all.

599   Woodrow Wilson was a leading scholar of British political history. He once made this judgment of Edmund Burke: "If you would be a leader of men, you must lead your own generation, not the next."

600   Count Alexis de Tocqueville, in his prophetic book on America in the 1840's, wrote that "a leader who is afraid to speak out . . . is unworthy of public trust."

601   May the Gods grant
                       Divine favor to our champion
                       Since justly he comes forward
                       A fighter for us.—*Aeschylus*

602   Mountains culminate in peaks and nations in men.—*José Martí*

603 Leaders have a significant role in creating the state of mind that is society.—*John Gardner*

604 The reward of the general is not a bigger tent, but command.—*Oliver Wendell Holmes*

605 A man who could not seduce men cannot save them either.—*Søren Kierkegaard*

606 Not to decide is to decide.—*Harvey Cox*

607 Energy in the executive is a leading character in the definition of good government.—*Alexander Hamilton*

608 Men are not led by being told what they do not know.—*Woodrow Wilson*

609 I sit here all day trying to persuade people to do the things they ought to have sense enough to do without my persuading them. That's all the powers of the President amount to.—*Harry S. Truman*

610 To seize the initiative even with risks and uncertainties—that is what I like to do.—*Charles de Gaulle*

611 Tribulation is to leaders what a furnace is to fine gold.—*Mary Queen of Scots*

612 Nothing gains estimation for a prince like great enterprises.—*Niccolò Machiavelli*

613 One sign of responsibility is the making of an intelligent analysis, not only of events that have occurred but of possibilities that might occur.—*Sidney Hook*

614 The nation's leaders must serve as symbols of the moral unity of society.—*John Gardner*

615 We need leaders of inspired idealism, leaders to whom are granted great visions, who dream greatly and strive to make their dreams come true, who can kindle the people with the fire from their burning souls.—*Theodore Roosevelt*

Liberalism

see HUMANITY;
also CONSERVATISM

616   The finest task of achieving justice will be done neither by
the Utopians who dream dreams of perfect brotherhood nor yet
by the cynics who believe that the self-interest of nations cannot
be overcome. It must be done by the realists who understand that
nations are selfish and will be so till the end of history, but that
none of us, no matter how selfish we may be, can be only selfish.
—*Reinhold Niebuhr*

617   Those who won our independence by revolution were not
cowards. They did not fear political change. They did not exalt
order at the cost of liberty.—*Louis Brandeis*

618   The liberal party is a party which believes that, as new
conditions and problems arise beyond the power of men and
women to meet as individuals, it becomes the duty of the government itself to find new remedies with which to meet them.—*Franklin D. Roosevelt*

619   Society can only pursue its normal course by means of a
certain progression of changes.—*Viscount Morley*

620   This country will not be a good place for any of us to live
in unless we make it a good place for all of us to live in.—*Theodore Roosevelt*

Liberty

see FREEDOM;
also REPRESSION

621   The law of liberty tends to abolish the reign of race over
race; of faith over faith and of class over class. This is not the
realization of a political idea; it is the discharge of a moral obligation.—*Lord Acton*

622   The true danger is when liberty is nibbled away for expedients and by parts.—*Edmund Burke*

623   Political liberty is a sign of moral and economic independence.—*George Santayana*

624   Liberty means responsibility. That's why most men dread it.—*George Bernard Shaw*

625   The people never give up their liberties but under some delusion.—*Edmund Burke*

Life

see CHALLENGE, SERVICE

626   Be inspired with the belief that life is a great and noble calling; not a mean and groveling thing that we are to shuffle through as we can, but an elevated and lofty destiny.—*William E. Gladstone*

627   To be poised against fatality to meet adverse conditions gracefully, is more than simple endurance; it is an act of aggression, a positive triumph.—*Thomas Mann*

628   That life is worth living is the most necessary of assumptions and were it not assumed, the most impossible of conclusions. —*José Ortega y Gasset*

629   I exhort you also to take part in the greatest combat, which is the combat of life and greater than every other earthly conflict. —*Plato*

630   I've never forgotten for long at a time that living is struggle. I know that every good and excellent thing in the world stands moment by moment on the razor-edge of danger and must be fought for. All I ask is the chance to build new worlds and God has always given us that second chance and has given us voices to guide us and the memory of our mistakes to warn us.—*Thornton Wilder*

631   The great majority of us are required to live a life of constant duplicity. Your health is bound to be affected if, day after

day, you say the opposite of what you feel, if you grovel before what you dislike, and rejoice at what brings you nothing but misfortune.—*Boris Pasternak*

632   Life is judged with all the blindness of life itself.—*George Santayana*

633   Life overflows its molds and the will outstrips its own universals.—*Learned Hand*

634   He who can take no interest in what is small, will take false interest in what is large.—*John Ruskin*

635   Life is like playing a violin solo in public and learning the instrument as one goes on.—*Samuel Butler*

636   If this life be not a real fight, in which something is eternally gained for the universe by success, it is not better than a game of private theatricals from which one may withdraw at will. —*William James*

637   Life is an offensive, directed against the repetitious mechanism of the universe.—*Alfred North Whitehead*

638   Life is a petty thing unless it is moved by the indomitable urge to extend its boundaries.—*José Ortega y Gasset*

639   Life is a roar of bargain and battle—but in the very heart of it there rises a mystical spiritual tone that gives meaning to the whole. It transmutes the dull details into romance.—*Oliver Wendell Holmes*

640   Life is the art of drawing sufficient conclusions from insufficient premises.—*Samuel Butler*

641   Existence is a strange bargain. Life owes little, we owe it everything. The only true happiness comes from squandering ourselves for a purpose.—*John Mason Brown*

642   We can do noble acts without ruling earth and sea.—*Aristotle*

643   Life's business being just the terrible choice.—*Robert Browning*

Materialism

see CIVILIZATION, DECLINE

644   We cannot hope to achieve salvation by worshipping the god of the standard of living.—*Robert Taft*

645   Things are in the saddle,
And ride mankind.—*Ralph Waldo Emerson*

646   The basic problem is that our civilization, which is a civilization of machines, can teach man everything except how to be a man.—*André Malraux*

647   The lust for comfort, that stealthy thing that enters the house as a guest and then becomes a host and then a master.—*Joseph Conrad*

648   Those who speak most of progress measure it by quantity and not by quality.—*George Santayana*

Medicine

see WELFARE

649   When Dr. Jonas Salk received a medal from President Eisenhower in 1956 for discovering polio vaccine, he said, "I feel that the greatest reward for doing is the opportunity to do more."

650   There are no such things as incurables, there are only things for which man has not found a cure.—*Bernard Baruch*

651   Care more for the individual patient than for the special features of the disease.—*Sir William Osler*

Mediocrity

see also EXCELLENCE

652   Prime Minister Otto von Bismarck once characterized Napoleon III with the words:

"He is a great unrecognized incapacity."

653   Senator Roman Hruska, who supported the ill-fated Judge Harrold Carswell for the Supreme Court, undermined his chances when he said, "Mediocrity deserves representation too."

Memorial

see GRATITUDE, REMEMBRANCE, SACRIFICE, SERVICE

654   James Russell Lowell eulogized the naturalist Louis Agassiz in more than five hundred lines, but came closest to catching the essence of the man in eleven words:
"His magic was not far to seek—he was so human!"

655   Cato, the Roman statesman, on observing that statues were being set up in honor of many, remarked, "I would rather people would ask, why is there *not* a statue to Cato, than why there is."

656   When Hamlet died, Horatio said:
"His life was gentle and the elements so mixed in him that nature might stand on its feet and say to all the world—'This was a man.'"

657   In the Boston-Irish political novel *The Last Hurrah* by Frank O'Connor, boss Skeffington is dying. His old enemy the cardinal is at his bedside. The cardinal piously says, "We can be sure he'd do things differently."
Skeffington answers, "Like hell I would."

658   A man's life, like a piece of tapestry, is made up of many strands which interwoven make a pattern. To separate a single one and look at it alone, not only destroys the whole, but gives the strand itself a false value.—*Learned Hand*

659   The deeds of just men never die.—*Aeschylus*

660   Faith is not taught by arguments. It is taught by lives.—*Archibald MacLeish*

661   Every man is son of his own work.—*Cervantes*

Negro

see BROTHERHOOD, POVERTY, PREJUDICE

662   In a short story by Chilean Nobel Prize winner Jorge Luis Borges, a Negro who wants to avenge the murder of his brother years before finally confronts the assassin. Says the white man, "I made you wait many days, but here I am." Says the Negro, "I'm getting used to waiting."

663   In 1840 a perceptive French commentator on America foresaw that the only problem that could trouble the American democracy was the failure to give the black population equal rights. Count Alexis de Tocqueville wrote:
   "If ever America undergoes great revolutions, they will be brought about by the presence of the black race on the soil of the United States; that is to say, they will owe their origin, not to the equality, but to the inequality, of condition."

664   In Mark Twain's *Huckleberry Finn,* Huck says about Jim: "I never seen such a nigger. If he got a notion in his head once, there warn't no getting it out again."

665   The only power blacks have is when they share and join that power with whites.—*Bayard Ruskin*

666   The Negro problem is not only America's greatest failure but also America's greatest opportunity for the future. If America should follow its own deepest convictions, its well-being at home would be increased directly. At the same time America's prestige and power abroad would rise.—*Gunnar Myrdal*

667   The Negro may wind up with a mouthful of civil rights, but an empty stomach and living in a hovel.—*Whitney Young*

668   We are confronted primarily with a moral issue. It is as old as the Scriptures, and is as clear as the American Constitution.—*John F. Kennedy*

669   We must learn to live together as brothers or perish together as fools.—*Martin Luther King, Jr.*

670   The Negro lives on a lonely island of poverty in the midst of a vast ocean of material prosperity and finds himself an exile in his own land.—*Martin Luther King, Jr.*

671   When we see society's failures—dropouts and dope addicts, petty thieves or prostitutes—we do not know whether they are Italian or English, Baptist or Orthodox. But we do know when they are Negro. So every Negro who fails confirms the voice of prejudice.—*Robert F. Kennedy*

672   The Negro American has been waiting upon voluntary action since 1776. He has found what other Americans have discovered: voluntary action has to be sparked by something stronger than prayers, patience, and lamentations. If the thirteen colonies had waited for voluntary action by England, this land today would be part of the British Commonwealth.—*Roy Wilkins*

673   I want to be the white man's brother, not his brother-in-law.—*Martin Luther King, Jr.*

Ordeal

674   When the French cleric and statesman Abbé Sieyès was asked what he did during the Reign of Terror by Robespierre, he replied, *"J'ai vecu"* (I survived).

Order

see JUSTICE, LAW;
also ANARCHY, REVOLUTION, VIOLENCE

675   When the Roman Emperor Marcus Aurelius was told by his mother, "You have made your authority too gentle and the rule of the empire less respected," he replied, "Yes, but I have made it more lasting and secure."

676   It is not our freedom that is in jeopardy, in the first instance; it is our public order. If that breaks down, freedom will be lost and so . . . will the prospect for greater justice.—*Eric Sevareid*

677   The balance of power within our society has turned dangerously against the peace forces.—*Walter Lippmann*

678   Peace itself means self-discipline at home and invulnerability abroad.—*George Santayana*

679   Order is the first desideratum for the simple reason that chaos means nonexistence.—*Reinhold Niebuhr*

680   Not every defeat of authority is a gain for individual freedom, nor every judicial rescue of a convict a victory for liberty.—*Robert Jackson*

681   Eternal vigilance is the price of order as well as liberty.—*Will Durant*

Patriotism

see AMERICA, HERITAGE

682   In his farewell address in 1796, President George Washington warned, "Guard against the postures of pretended patriotism."

683   The wife of General George Patton, when asked how she put up with having to move so much, replied, "My home is always under the flag."

684   In the House of Commons, a Tory member named Burdett declared that there was nothing more odious than the cant of patriotism. To which Lord Russell replied:
    "The cant of patriotism was no doubt very odious, but there was something even more odious and that was the recant of patriotism."

685   In one of his last public speeches, General Douglas MacArthur told the young cadets assembled in his honor on the plain: "In the evening of my memory, always I come back to West Point. Always there echoes and re-echoes in my ears—Duty—Honor—Country. . . . When I cross the river my last conscious thoughts will be of the Corps—and the Corps—and the Corps."

686   As a tribute to one's forefathers, the words of Ecclesiastes attributed to King Solomon are unsurpassed:
    Let us now praise famous men and our fathers that begat us. The Lord hath wrought great glory by them, through his great

power from the beginning. Such as did bear rule in their kingdoms, men renowned for their power, giving counsel by their understanding, and declaring prophecies: leaders of the people by their counsels. . . But these were merciful men whose righteousness hath not been forgotten, with their seed shall continually remain a good inheritance, and their children are within the covenant. Their seed stands fast and their children for their sakes. Their seed shall remain forever and their glory shall not be blotted out. Their bodies are buried in peace but their name liveth for evermore. The people will tell of their wisdom and the congregation will show forth their praise.

687   Patriotism is doing anything to serve one's country in whatever way it needs most to be served at any given point in history.—*Theodore Hesburgh*

688   Nationalist pride . . . can be a substitute for self-respect. Hence the paradox that when government policies or historical accidents make the attainment and maintenance of individual respect difficult, the nationalist spirit of the people becomes more ardent and more extreme.—*Eric Hoffer*

689   The man who has nothing to do for his country cannot love it.—*John Stuart Mill*

690   I venture to suggest that patriotism is not short and frenzied outbursts of emotion, but the tranquil and steady dedication of a lifetime.—*Adlai Stevenson*

691   A man's feet should stand in his own country, but his eyes should survey the world.—*George Santayana*

692   I should like to be able to love my country and still love justice.—*Albert Camus*

Peace

see FOREIGN POLICY, INTERNATIONALISM;
also WAR

693   In 1941 by Executive Order President Franklin D. Roosevelt took the eagle on the U.S. Seal and turned its head toward the olive branch, away from the arrows.

694   In their historic meeting in Germany in 1807, Napoleon told Czar Alexander of Russia:

"If they want peace, nations should avoid the pinpricks that precede cannon-shots."

695   In 1959, President Dwight D. Eisenhower impassionedly told Prime Minister Harold Macmillan,

"I think that people want peace so much that one of these days government had better get out of their way and let them have it."

696   In 750 B.C. the prophet Micah wrote those beautiful words of peace:

And they shall beat their swords into ploughshares, and their spears into pruning hooks; nation shall not lift up a sword against nation, neither shall they learn war any more.

697   In 1945, Bernard Baruch presented to the United Nations a proposal for multilateral disarmament. He opened his remarks with these words: "We are here to choose between the quick and the dead."

698   War is an invention of the human mind. The human mind also can invent peace.—*Norman Cousins*

699   Peace cannot be kept by force. It can only be achieved by understanding.—*Albert Einstein*

700   What, then, is the objective of those who are at the helm of government, which they should never lose sight of, toward which they ought to set their course? It is what is best and most desirable for all good, sound, prosperous citizens: namely, peace with dignity.—*Cicero*

701   Mankind must put an end to war, or war will put an end to mankind.—*John F. Kennedy*

702   Peace hath its victories, no less renowned than war.—*John Milton*

703   To be prepared for war is one of the most effective means of preserving peace.—*George Washington*

704   We have become nuclear giants but ethical infants; we know more about war than we know about peace, more about killing than we know about living.—*Omar Bradley*

705   The peace we seek is nothing less than the practice and fulfillment of our whole faith. It signifies more than stalking the gains, easing the sorrow of war. More than escape from death, it is a way of life. More than a haven for the enemy, it is a hope for the brave.—*Dwight D. Eisenhower*

706   We have the power to make this the best generation of mankind in the history of the world—or to make it the last.—*John F. Kennedy*

707   You don't start a world war when a democracy throws its weight around facing a bully. World wars are started when the democracies are too unprepared, too frightened, too cowardly, too reasonable, too tired, or too humanitarian.—*Eric Hoffer*

Perseverance

see RESOLUTION

708   Once when the pianist Jan Paderewski played before Queen Victoria, she said, "Mr. Paderewski, you are a genius."
   He replied, "Before I was a genius, Your Majesty, I was a drudge."

709   In the British Museum one can see seventy-five drafts of Thomas Gray's poem, "Elegy Written in a Country Churchyard." Gray didn't like the first way he wrote it, nor the second nor the third. He was not satisfied till he revised it seventy-five times.

710   Abraham Lincoln once commented on General Grant's fighting tenacity to General Butler, saying, "When General Grant once gets possessed of a place he seems to hang on to it as if he had inherited it."

Planning

see LEADERSHIP

711   In his *Epistles* the Roman statesman and philosopher Seneca writes:
   "Our plans miscarry because they have no aim. When a man

does not know what harbor he is making for, no wind is the right wind."

712   In his Gospel, Luke records Jesus Christ's parable of the tower:
"For which of you, intending to build a tower, sitteth not down first, and counteth the cost, whether he have sufficient to finish it?"

713   Scipio Africanus, the Roman general who conquered Carthage, once said, "In military affairs, 'I didn't think of it' is a disgraceful phrase."

714   As Cervantes' Don Quixote tells Sancho Panza:
"Forewarned, forearmed—to be prepared is half the battle."

715   We must ask where we are and whither we are tending.—*Abraham Lincoln*

716   When the plans themselves are bad, there can be no expectations that leave any place for courage.—*Sophocles*

717   Make no little plans; they have no magic to stir men's blood.—*Daniel Burnham*

718   It is better to have a bad plan than to have no plan at all.—*Charles de Gaulle*

719   Nothing is more terrible than activity without insight.—*Thomas Carlyle*

720   Planning itself is one of the most progressive steps the human race has taken. But it can be a curse if it is "blind" planning in which man abdicates his own decisions, value judgment, and responsibility. If it is alive, responsive, "open" planning in which the human ends are in full awareness and guiding the planning process, it will be a blessing.—*Erich Fromm*

721   To be in heaven is to steer—to be in hell is to drift.—*George Bernard Shaw*

722   Quite as important as legislation is vigilant oversight of administration.—*Woodrow Wilson*

723   Style is the ultimate morality of the mind. The administra-

tor with a sense of style hates waste; the engineer with a sense of style economizes his material; the artisan with a sense of style prefers good work.—*Alfred North Whitehead*

Politics

see GOVERNMENT, CITIZENSHIP

724   On the Ivory Coast, then part of French West Africa, there was elected some years ago a distinguished Negro lawyer as a senator to Paris. The senator returned to his constituency in 1950 to do some electioneering, and disappeared out in the bush. All efforts to trace him failed. Three years later he was officially declared dead by a court which, on inspecting evidence, decided that he had been eaten by cannibals.

Though many politicians have claimed to have been roasted by their constituents, in this case it was literally true.

725   In Shakespeare's *Henry VI,* the opportunistic Gloucester, the future Richard III, cynically espouses his philosophy:
"I'll play the orator as well as Nestor,
Deceive more slily than Ulysses could,
And like a Sinon, take another Troy.
I can add colours to the chameleon,
Change shapes with Proteus for advantages,
And set the murderous Machiavel to school."

726   In 1968, Congressman John Ashbrook of Ohio rose to plead with his fellow Republicans to allow at least some of the Ohio delegates to be guided by their consciences rather than being dictated to by the governor and the party organization.

Replied a delegate named Craven, in a political aphorism which will long outlive the man who uttered it, "Conscience is for church people, not for politicians."

727   As Shakespeare's King Lear says, "Get thee glass eyes and like a scurvy politician seem to see things thou dost not."

728   Don't look down on the politician for never having met a payroll if you never have carried a precinct.—*Theodore N. Sorensen*

729   We must not say that a man who takes no interest in politics minds his own business; we say he has no business here at all. —*Pericles*

730   An honorable profession calls forth the chance for responsibility and the opportunity for achievement; against these measures politics is truly an exciting adventure.—*Robert F. Kennedy*

731   Politics is like booze and women: dangerous but incomparably exciting.—*James Reston*

732   Politics should be the part-time profession of every citizen. —*Dwight D. Eisenhower*

733   In our time the destiny of man presents its meaning in political terms.—*Thomas Mann*

734   Governments are what politicians make them.—*Woodrow Wilson*

735   A new science of politics is needed for a new world.— *Alexis de Tocqueville*

736   State business is a cruel trade; good nature is a bungler in it.—*Lord Halifax*

737   Politics is perhaps the only profession for which no preparation is thought necessary.—*Robert Louis Stevenson*

738   Whenever a man has cast a longing eye on office, a rottenness begins in his conduct.—*Thomas Jefferson*

739   He knows nothing; he thinks he knows everything—that clearly points to a political career.—*George Bernard Shaw*

740   I am not a politician and my other habits are good.— *Artemus Ward*

741   Politicians neither love nor hate; interest, not sentiment governs them.—*G. K. Chesterton*

742   Politics is no ocean voyage or military campaign. It is not a public chore to be got over with. It's a way of life.—*Plutarch*

743   Don't ever lose touch with your constituency, don't ever mistake the voice of the clubman and the voice of the pressman in

London for the voice of the country. It is the country that has returned you. It is the country that will judge you.—*Stanley Baldwin*

744   Romantic ruthlessness is no nearer to real politics than is romantic self-abnegation.—*Alfred North Whitehead*

745   All politics is the rivalry of organized minorities; the voters are the bleachers who cheer the victors and jeer the defeats but do not otherwise contribute to the result.—*Will Durant*

746   One of the shallowest disdains is the sneer against the professional politician.—*Felix Frankfurter*

747   If politics in America is not to become the art of the impossible, the limits of politics must be perceived and the province of moral philosophy greatly expanded.—*Daniel Patrick Moynihan*

Population

see POVERTY

748   There was an old woman who lived in a shoe.
She had so many children she didn't know what to do.
She gave them broth, without any bread,
And whipped them all soundly, and sent them to bed.
—*English Nursery Rhyme*

749   In Lewis Carroll's *Alice in Wonderland,* the White Queen says to Alice: "What's one and one and one and one and one and one and one and one and one?"
And Alice replies: "I don't know. I lost count."

750   We have been God-like in our planned breeding of our domesticated plants and animals, but we have been rabbit-like in our unplanned breeding of ourselves.—*Arnold Toynbee*

Poverty

see CITY, NEGRO, POPULATION, WELFARE

751   When Buddha as a youth went for the first time from his father's estate to the streets of Calcutta, he saw a leper and asked his driver, "What is that?"

The reply was, "Think nothing of it, Master, that is the way of life."

Next he saw a blind man begging for alms and again to his question came, "Think nothing of it, Master, that is the way of life."

And, finally, he saw a corpse lying in the road being consumed by flies and vultures. Again the driver's answer was, "Think nothing of it, Master, that is the way of life."

But Buddha said, "No, that must not be the way of life." It was then that he started on his life of service.

752   *Sal Si Puedes* is the title of a book by Peter Matthiessen. It was the name given to the *barrio,* or ghetto, in San Jose, California, in which Cesar Chavez was born. It means in Spanish, "Escape if you can."

753   In Charles Dickens's *Christmas Carol,* Scrooge suffers a terrible vision of the two children, the boy called Ignorance, the girl called Want.

"Have they no refuge or resource?" cried Scrooge.

"Are there no prisons?" said the Spirit. "Are there no workhouses?"

754   You don't have to look for distress; it is screaming at you. —*Samuel Beckett*

755   Wealth is conspicuous, but poverty hides.—*James Reston*

756   The earliest prophet whose writings we may suppose ourselves to possess is Amos, the peasant poet. In 750 B.C., he saw and denounced the crimes of exploiters:

> . . . You men who crush the humble, and oppress the poor, only muttering, "When will the new moon come, that we may sell our grain? When will the Sabbath be over, that we may sell our wheat?" Small you make your measures, large your weights. You cheat by tampering with the scales—and all to buy up innocent folk, to buy up the needy for a pair of sandals and to sell them the very refuse of your grain.

757   Benjamin Disraeli described the "haves" and "have nots" as "two nations between whom there is no intercourse and no sym-

pathy; who are so ignorant of each other's habits, thoughts, and feelings, as if they were dwellers in different zones or inhabitants of different planets."

758   In a society that has discovered the "know-how" of Amalthea's cornucopia, the always ugly unequality in the distribution of the world's goods in ceasing to be a practical necessity has become a moral enormity.—*Arnold Toynbee*

759   Poverty is the parent of revolution and crime.—*Aristotle*

760   Poverty has many roots, but the taproot is ignorance.—*Lyndon B. Johnson*

761   Man holds in his mortal hands the power to abolish all forms of human poverty and, indeed, all forms of human life.—*John F. Kennedy*

762   A decent provision for the poor is the best measure of civilization.—*Samuel Johnson*

763   Poverty demoralizes.—*Ralph Waldo Emerson*

764   The slum is the measure of civilization.—*Jacob Riis*

765   Must the hunger become anger and the anger fury before anything will be done?—*John Steinbeck*

766   A hungry man listens not to reason nor cares for justice nor is bent by any prayers.—*Seneca*

767   For every talent that poverty has stimulated it has blighted a hundred.—*John Gardner*

768   Modern poverty is not the poverty that was blest in the Sermon on the Mount.—*George Bernard Shaw*

Power

see GOVERNMENT, LEADERSHIP

769   As Isabella says in Shakespeare's *Measure for Measure:*
"Oh, it is excellent to have a giant's strength. But it is tyrannous to use it like a giant."

770   In John Steinbeck's *Short Reign of Pippin IV,* the king says: "Power does not corrupt. Fear corrupts, perhaps the fear of a loss of power."

771   As for the men in power, they are so anxious to establish the myth of infallibility that they do their utmost to ignore truth. —*Boris Pasternak*

772   Power is poison.—*Henry Adams*

773   Constant experience shows us that every man invested with power is apt to abuse it, and to carry his authority as far as it will go.—*Baron de Montesquieu*

774   No extraordinary power should be lodged in any one individual.—*Thomas Paine*

775   Power intoxicates men. When a man is intoxicated by alcohol, he can recover, but when intoxicated by power, he seldom recovers.—*James Byrnes*

776   The finest combination in the world is power and mercy. The worst combination in the world is weakness and strife.—*Winston Churchill*

777   Absolute power is partial to simplicity. It wants simple solutions, simple definitions. It sees in complication a product of weakness—the tortuous path compromise must follow. There is thus a certain similarity between the pattern of extremism and that of absolute power.—*Eric Hoffer*

778   Power does not corrupt men; but fools, if they get into a position of power, corrupt power.—*George Bernard Shaw*

Prejudice

see NEGRO, POVERTY;
also BROTHERHOOD

779   When the enemies of John Milton mocked his blindness, the poet with great heat replied:
    "I prefer my blindness to yours. Yours is sunk into your deepest

senses blinding your minds. Mine takes from me only the color and surface of things, but does not take away from the mind's contemplation what is in those things true and constant."

780   Ignorance is less remote from truth than prejudice.— *Denis Diderot*

781   The mind of a bigot is like the pupil of the eye; the more light you pour on it, the more it will contract.—*Oliver Wendell Holmes*

782   The people who are the most bigoted are the people who have no convictions at all.—*G. K. Chesterton*

783   The most certain test by which we judge whether a country is really free is the amount of security enjoyed by minorities. —*Lord Acton*

784   I dart a contemptuous look at the stately monuments of superstition.—*Edward Gibbon*

785   Let us hope that the dark clouds of racial prejudice will soon pass away, that the deep fog of misunderstanding will be lifted from our fear-drenched communities, and that in some not too distant tomorrow the radiant stars of love and brotherhood will shine over our great nation with all their scintillating beauty. —*Martin Luther King, Jr.*

786   The prejudices of ignorance are more easily removed than the prejudices of interest; the first are blindly adopted, the second willfully preferred.—*George Bancroft*

787   Racism is the snobbery of the poor.—*Raymond Aron*

788   It is never too late to give up your prejudices.—*Henry David Thoreau*

789   I am not a know-nothing. . . . As a nation we began by declaring, "All men are created equal." We now practically read it "All men are created equal except Negroes, foreigners, and Catholics." When it comes to this I should prefer emigrating to a country where there is made no pretense of loving liberty; to Rus-

sia, for instance, whose despotism can be taken pure and without the base alloy of hypocrisy.—*Abraham Lincoln*

790   Remember that when you say "I will have none of this exile and this stranger for his face is not like my face and his speech is strange," you have denied America with that word.—*Stephen Vincent Benét*

Principles

see VALUES;
also EXPEDIENCY

791   Man is what he believes.—*Anton Chekhov*

792   Belief consists in accepting the affirmations of the soul. —*Ralph Waldo Emerson*

793   The tragedy of life is what dies inside a man while he lives. —*Albert Schweitzer*

Problem

see SOLUTION, URGENCY

794   A disciple of Confucius said to the Master on one occasion when the reigning prince of a certain state was negotiating for Confucius to enter his service: "The prince is waiting, sir, to entrust the government of the country to you. Now what do you consider the first thing to be done?"

"If I must begin," answered Confucius, "I would begin by defining 'things.' "

795   When Heavyweight Champion Joe Louis was interviewed before his second fight with Billy Conn, he was asked how he would handle Conn's back-pedaling tactics in the ring.

Replied Joe, "He can run, but he can't hide."

796   Dean Acheson confided to Premier Salazar of Portugal in Lisbon in 1951: "When I became Secretary of State, an old

friend said to me, 'Always remember the future comes one day at a time.' "

797   The word "problem" comes from the Greek word *probouleuma*, which meant a bill of great urgency ready for immediate passage in the legislature of Athens.

798   In Lewis Carroll's *Alice in Wonderland*, we remember the Mad Hatter describing the situation to Alice as "much of a muchness."

799   In Japanese there is a word for cutting through a problem to the core. It is *wari kiru*.

800   Dean Acheson, who served as Undersecretary of State when George C. Marshall was Secretary of State, once quoted one of the general's famous rules:
"Don't fight the problem; decide it."

801   Robert Lovett, who was Secretary of Defense under Harry Truman, once quoted a Spanish proverb:
"No quiero el queso sino salir de la ratonera"—"I don't want the cheese. I just want to get out of the trap."

802   As Léon Gambetta advised after the German defeat of France in 1871, "Let us study our misfortunes and go back to the causes."

803   As the defeated British regiments marched past the files of French and American troops at Yorktown, the British bands, in detached resignation, played "The World Upside Down."

804   "Kefloffle," in the Cockney argot of London, means "bungled opportunity."

805   In 1968, in the midst of Parisian disturbances, someone put a poster over the door to the science faculty building at the University of Sorbonne. The poster read: "Be a realist. Do the impossible."

806   We face difficulties which are big with portent, and uncertain of solution.—*Learned Hand*

807   It is said, reap where you have sown. That is a hard rule, a stern rule, and we accept it. But we are not reaping where we have sown, we are reaping where others have sown, where they have sown weeds, as well as grain.—*Winston Churchill*

808   The worst, the most corrupting of lies are problems poorly stated.—*Georges Bernanos*

809   The whole dignity of human endeavor is thus bound up with historic issues.—*George Santayana*

810   Proximate solutions to man's insoluble problems.—*Reinhold Neibuhr*

811   We are confronted by a condition, not a theory.—*Grover Cleveland*

812   There are nowadays professors of philosophy, but not philosophers. Yet it is admirable to profess because it was once admirable to live. To be a philosopher is not merely to have subtle thoughts, nor even to found a school, but so to love wisdom as to live according to its dictates, a life of simplicity, independence, magnanimity, and trust. It is to solve some of the problems of life, not only theoretically, but practically.—*Henry David Thoreau*

813   In such a strait the wisest may well be perplexed and the boldest staggered.—*Edmund Burke*

814   Out of intense complexities, intense simplicities emerge. —*Winston Churchill*

815   These are not the days of miracles, and I suppose it will be granted that I am not to expect a direct revelation. I must study the plain physical facts of the case, ascertain what is possible, and learn what appears to be wise and right.—*Abraham Lincoln*

816   We live in the midst of alarms; anxiety beclouds the future; we expect some new disaster with each newspaper we read. —*Abraham Lincoln*

817   Probe the earth and see where your main roots run.— *Henry David Thoreau*

Progress

see CHANGE, REFORM;
also PREJUDICE, REACTIONARY

818   When Abraham Lincoln signed the *Emancipation Proclamation,* a great many letters protesting it reached the White House. To one of these Lincoln replied, "I am a slow walker. But I never walk back. . . ."

819   The world is advancing; advance with it.—*Giuseppi Mazzini*

820   Our problems are man-made, therefore they can be solved by man. And man can be as big as he wants. No problem of human destiny is beyond human beings. Man's reason and spirit have often solved the seemingly insolvable and we believe they can do it again.—*John F. Kennedy*

821   Fundamental progress has to do with the reinterpretation of basic ideas.—*Alfred North Whitehead*

822   Progressiveness means not standing still when everything else is moving.—*Woodrow Wilson*

823   Be progressive. A great democracy has got to be progressive, or it will soon cease to be great or a democracy.—*Theodore Roosevelt*

Public Office

see GOVERNMENT, LEADERSHIP, RESPONSIVENESS

824   When a White House aide told President Nixon he would relay a request "to the appropriate mechanism," the President proceeded to reminisce about a visit he had made to a nation behind the Iron Curtain in 1959.
"There was a steel mill on the itinerary," he said. "The diplomat who was my escort officer—a brilliant fellow—turned me over to the plant manager for the usual guided tour. The manager was

especially proud of the new machinery in the plant, and he told me all about what it cost and how it speeded up the process. He got a little impatient when I stopped to shake hands with the workers around whatever machine he was showing off. In the car on the way back from the mill, the diplomat said something I've always remembered. 'It's not hard to find men who understand machinery,' he said. 'Our trouble is we don't have enough men who understand men.' "

825   On September 12, 1912, Governor Woodrow Wilson of New Jersey, the Democratic nominee for the Presidency, addressed the Democratic state committee and the Democratic county chairmen of New York at Syracuse. Wilson's theme was "American Politics." He said,

"I'll tell you frankly, the people of the United States are tired of politics. They are sick of politics. They long, down in the bottom of their natures, for a release from everything except that which makes the public service look like public duty and legislation look like the translation of the public need into public act."

826   The first and essential quality towards being a statesman is to have a public spirit.—*Sir Richard Steele*

827   For titles do not reflect honor on men but rather men on their titles.—*Niccolò Machiavelli*

828   We have been taught to regard a representative of the people as a sentinel on the watch-tower of liberty.—*Daniel Webster*

829   Your representative owes you not only his industry, but also his judgment, and he betrays instead of serving you if he sacrifices it to your opinion.—*Edmund Burke*

Public Opinion

see EXPEDIENCY, LEADERSHIP, RESPONSIVENESS

830   To serve the public interest is not the same as being a servant of public opinion.—*Sidney Hook*

831   It is sometimes easier to face a cannon than public opinion.—*Edward Gibbon*

832   The masses of men are very difficult to excite on bare grounds of self-interest; most easy if a bold orator tells them confidently they are wronged.—*Walter Bagehot*

833   In proportion as the structure of a government gives force to public opinion, it is essential that the public opinion be enlightened.—*George Washington*

834   We forgot to make ourselves intelligent when we made ourselves sovereign.—*Will Durant*

835   Public opinion is a compound of folly, weakness, prejudice, wrong feeling, right feeling, obstinacy, and newspaper paragraphs.—*Sir Robert Peel*

Purpose

see COMMITMENT, PLANNING, PRINCIPLES, VALUES

836   In *Alice in Wonderland,* Alice asks the Cheshire Cat for directions: "Would you tell me, please, which way I ought to go from here?"
    "That depends a good deal on where you want to get to," says the cat.
    "I don't much care where . . . ," said Alice.
    "Then it doesn't matter which way you go," says the cat.

837   John Gardner wrote that the Mayan civilization failed because it had no great ideal to sustain it. It had everything but a sense of purpose and mission.

838   Mark Van Doren was lunching with some of his Amherst students who asked him what they should do with their lives. "Whatever you want," said Van Doren, "just so long as you don't miss the main thing!"
    "What is that?"
    "Your lives," said Van Doren.

839   In Arthur Miller's *Death of a Salesman,* Biff says about his father, "He never knew who he was."

840   "We know what we are," said Ophelia in Shakespeare's *Hamlet,* "but we know not what we may become."

841   A man's true greatness lies in the consciousness of an honest purpose in life.—*Marcus Aurelius*

842   Our task now is not to fix the blame for the past, but to fix the course for the future.—*John F. Kennedy*

843   Great minds have purposes, others have wishes.—*Washington Irving*

844   What is the use of living, if it be not to strive for noble causes and to make this muddled world a better place to live in after we are gone.—*Winston Churchill*

845   I have brought myself by long meditation to the conviction that a human being with a settled purpose must accomplish it and that nothing can resist a will which will stake even existence upon its fulfillment.—*Abraham Lincoln*

846   The sense of uselessness is the severest shock which our system can sustain.—*Thomas Huxley*

847   The great use of a life is to spend it for something that outlasts it.—*William James*

848   The great society is a place where men are more concerned with the quality of their goals than the quantity of their goods.—*Lyndon B. Johnson*

849   Our nation is commissioned by history to be either an observer of freedom's failure or the cause of its success. Our overriding obligation in the period ahead is to fulfill the world's hope by fulfilling our own faith.—*John F. Kennedy*

850   We had best look our times and lands searchingly in the face.—*Walt Whitman*

851   Neither man nor nation can exist without a sublime idea.— *Fëdor Dostoevski*

852   American life and American society need a most critical examination from the perspectives of moral and political philosophy. How does our pursuit of affluence relate to our pursuit of happiness? What are the individual's rights and duties in this new and complex society we are creating? How can we reconcile our commitment to social equality with our commitment to personal liberty?—*Irving Kristol*

853   The bond of American union has not been piety and reverence for the past, but a conviction of purpose and of the destiny it would bring for posterity.—*Walter Lippmann*

854   My thesis is that to affirm the ultimate ends—as every public man does in almost every speech—is not a substitute for, is not the equivalent of, declaring our national purpose and of leading the nation. These affirmations are like standing up when "The Star-Spangled Banner" is being played and then doing nothing further about anything; they beg the question, which is not whither the nation should go, but how it should get there.—*Walter Lippmann*

Question

see LIFE, PURPOSE

855   Gertrude Stein, the writer, was asked, as she lay dying, by her friend Alice Toklas, "What is the answer?"
Gertrude replied, "What is the question?"

Radicals

see EXTREMISTS, REVOLUTION;
also CHANGE, CONSERVATISM, LIBERALISM

856   The sterile radical is basically . . . conservative. He is afraid to let go of the ideas and beliefs he picked up in his youth lest his life be seen as empty and wasted.—*Eric Hoffer*

857   The protestors are fired by their sense of moral righteousness. They feel they have learned from experience that it is neces-

sary to be loud and demonstrative to get results. It is this behavior that compels attention and strikes fear for the very stability of society.—*John D. Rockefeller 3rd*

858   The surest way to work up a crusade in favor of some good cause is to promise people that they will have a chance of maltreating someone . . . to be able the destroy with good conscience, to be able to behave badly and call their behavior "righteous indignation"—this is the height of psychological luxury, the most delicious of moral treats.—*Aldous Huxley*

859   Despite appearances, the protestor is usually not where the action is. The open and unfrequented path is more often to be formed within the system. You do not have to remind me how difficult it is to remain an individual to preserve independence and objectivity in thought, to resist not the pressure but the temptation to conform. And I admit that most will not remain, preserve, resist—but the few who do will make the difference, will find their paths not crowded. And the rest of us will accord them an immortality of sorts.—*J. Irwin Miller*

860   Too much reliance is placed in noisy demonstrations . . . they excite prejudice and close the avenues to sober reason.—*Abraham Lincoln*

861   The dignity of truth is lost with much protest.—*Ben Jonson*

862   The liberty of the individual must thus far be limited; he must not make himself a nuisance to other people.—*John Stuart Mill*

Reactionary

see PREJUDICE;
also CHANGE, PROGRESS

863   We remember the old story of how King Canute futilely ordered the waves to roll back and not overwhelm his throne in the sand.

864   Two British soldiers died in the skirmish at Concord Bridge in 1775. Their tomb, now part of the general shrine, bears a quatrain beginning:

> They came three thousand miles and died,
> To keep the past upon its throne . . .

865   The last sentence of F. Scott Fitzgerald's *The Great Gatsby* reads:
"And we beat on, in darkened boats against the current into the past."

866   Every progressive spirit is opposed by a thousand men appointed to guard the past . . . the least that the most timid among us can do is not to add to the immense deadweight that nature drives along.—*Maurice Maeterlinck*

867   The reactionaries have been winning the battles and losing the war.—*Walter Lippmann*

868   The march of the human mind is slow.—*Edmund Burke*

869   Loyalty to a petrified opinion never yet broke a chain or freed a human soul.—*Mark Twain*

Realism

see REASON;
also EXTREMISTS, REVOLUTION

870   Sir Thomas More wrote a book about an ideal country. The name of the book was *Utopia,* which in Greek means "no place."

871   In the play *The Rainmaker,* the character Starbuck says, "Nothing is ever as good when I get it in my hand as when I got it in my head."

872   There is a fable from Aesop about the astrologer who kept looking at the stars as he walked—so that he eventually fell into a hole.

873   An acre in Middlesex is better than a principality in Utopia.—*Thomas Macaulay*

874   The whole art of politics consists in directing rationally the irrationalities of men.—*Reinhold Niebuhr*

875   Reality is always more conservative than ideology.— *Raymond Aron*

Reason

see FACTS, KNOWLEDGE, REALISM;
also EXTREMISTS

876   There is an old Finnish drinking toast that goes "Farewell to Reason."

877   When the Greek philosophers found that the square root of two is not a rational number, they celebrated the discovery by sacrificing one hundred oxen.

878   There is a horrendous but moving etching by Goya called "The Sleep of Reason Generates Monsters."

879   There is a story that the town of Franklin, Massachusetts, was named in honor of Benjamin Franklin during the time that the distinguished American was still living. The townspeople wrote a letter to him and said, "We have named our town after you and we should like a donation of a sum of money from you in order that we may put a bell in the town hall steeple." Benjamin Franklin wrote, "I am very much honored, very glad indeed to send you a sum of money, only don't buy a bell with it. Buy a public library, because I have always preferred sense to sound."

Reform

see CHANGE, PROGRESS, REVOLUTION;
also REACTIONARY

880   We remember in Matthew's Gospel how Christ, after the Sermon on the Mount, explained to the followers of John the

Baptist, "Neither do men put new wine into old bottles or else the bottles break."

881   The classic example of fake reform is the story of Prince Potëmkin taking Catherine the Great on a tour and showing her the painted house fronts of empty shells as a representation of progress.

882   On passing the Reform Bill in 1866, Prime Minister Gladstone answered Disraeli's attack with these words: "You cannot fight against the future. Time is on our side. The great social forces which move onward in their might and majesty and which the tumult of your debates does not for a moment impede or disturb . . . are against you."

883   In Plutarch's *Lives,* the Roman leader Marius is pictured describing the risk of radical reform: "I see the cure is not worth the pain."

884   The hole and the patch should be commensurate.—*Thomas Jefferson*

885   We think we are on the right road to improvement because we are making experiments.—*Benjamin Franklin*

886   No reforms come easy; even the most obvious will have its entrenched enemies. Each one is carried to us on the bent and weary backs of patient, dedicated men and women.—*Adlai Stevenson*

887   A reform is a correction of abuses; a revolution is a transfer of power.—*Edward Bulwer-Lytton*

888   The responsible critic comes to understand the complex machinery by which change must be accomplished, finds the key points of leverage, identifies feasible alternatives and measures his work by real results.—*John Gardner*

889   The small reform may become the enemy of the great one. —*Viscount Morley*

890   We must reform if we would conserve.—*Franklin D. Roosevelt*

891   He that will not apply new remedies must expect new evils, for time is the greatest innovator.—*Francis Bacon*

892   There is nothing more difficult to take in hand, more perilous to conduct, or more uncertain in its success than to take the lead in the introduction of a new order of things.—*Niccolò Machiavelli*

893   New opinions are always suspected and usually opposed, for no other reason than because they are not already common.—*John Locke*

894   I say, beware of all enterprises that require new clothes and not rather a new wearer of clothes.—*Henry David Thoreau*

895   As the problems are new, we must disenthrall ourselves from the past.—*Abraham Lincoln*

896   To reform means to shatter one form and to create another; but the two sides of this act are not always equally intended nor equally successful.—*Alexis de Tocqueville*

897   Twentieth-century institutions are caught in a savage cross-fire between uncritical lovers and unloving critics. On the one side, those who loved their institutions tended to smother them in an embrace of death, loving their rigidities more than their promise, shielding them from life-giving criticisms. On the other side, there rose a breed of critics without love, skilled in demolition but untutored in the arts by which human institutions are nurtured, strengthened and made to flourish.—*John Gardner*

898   There are a thousand hacking at the branches of evil to one who is striking at its root.—*Henry David Thoreau*

Religion

see FAITH

899   The Quaker leader George Fox once exclaimed, "Dost thou call the steeple-house the church? No, the church is the people."

900   Let us picture for a moment what a reborn church would be. A life, not a creed, would be its test; what a man does, not what he professes; what he is, not what he has. What the world craves today is a more spiritual and less formal religion. I plead not for a modification of form, but for its subordination to the spirit, not for the abolishing of ordinances, but for their voluntary rather than obligatory observations.—*John D. Rockefeller, Jr.*

901   Science without religion is lame; religion without science is blind.—*Albert Einstein*

902   We have just enough religion to make us hate. But not enough to make us love one another.—*Jonathan Swift*

903   What shall we do to be saved? In the life of the spirit put the secular superstructure back onto religious foundations.—*Arnold Toynbee*

904   To celebrate the person today, religion will have to become more, not less, political. Churches will have to expose governmental programs that increase people's dependency and deepen their sense of powerlessness.—*Harvey Cox*

Remembrance

see MEMORIAL

905   *You Can't Go Home Again* is the title of one of Thomas Wolfe's greatest books.

906   In the heart of each man there is contrived, by desperate devices, a magical island. . . . We place it in the past or future for safety, for we dare not locate it in the present. . . . We call it memory or a vision to lend it solidity, but it is neither, really; it is the outcome of our sadness, and of our disgust with the world that we have made.—*E. M. Forster*

907   God gave us memory that we might have roses in December.—*James Barrie*

Renewal

see BEGINNING, FUTURE, VISION

908   In Swahili, the word *kwacha* means "the glitter of a new day."

909   Aristotle was once asked what hope is. His answer was, "The dream of a waking man."

910   Let us not go over the old ground, let us rather prepare for what is to come.—*Cicero*

911   The new circumstances under which we are placed call for new words, new phrases, and for the transfer of old words to new objects.—*Thomas Jefferson*

912   Methinks I see in my mind a noble and puissant nation rousing herself like a strong man after a sleep, and shaking her invincible locks.—*John Milton*

913   The dogmas of the quiet past are inadequate to the stormy present. The occasion is piled high with difficulty and we must rise with the occasion. As our case is now, so we must think anew and act anew.—*Abraham Lincoln*

914   Burn off my rusts, and my deformity.—*John Donne*

915   We are witnessing a renaissance of public spirit, a reawakening of sober public opinion, a revival of power of the people, the beginning of an age of thoughtful reconstruction . . . with the new age we shall show a new spirit. We shall serve justice and candor and all things that make for the right.—*Woodrow Wilson*

Repression

see also FREEDOM

916   When Bishop Walsh returned to America after twenty years of imprisonment in Red China, he said to his welcoming neighbors in Cumberland, Maryland, "It is a double privilege.

First, I get to breathe the bracing air of freedom, and second, I get to feel the warm atmosphere of my home town."

917   As the character in George Orwell's *1984* states: "A party member lives from birth to death under the eye of the Thought Police. Even when he is alone, he can never be sure that he is alone. Wherever he may be, asleep or awake, working or resting . . ."

918   Bad laws are the worst sort of tyranny.—*Edmund Burke*

919   Repression is the seed of revolution.—*Daniel Webster*

920   A nation may loose its liberties in a day and not miss them in a century.—*Baron de Montesquieu*

921   And lawlessness rules the laws, and men do not strive together.—*Euripides*

Resolution

see COMMITMENT, PERSEVERANCE

922   As the Apostle Paul wrote to the small Christian community of Galatians in Asia Minor, "Let us not be weary in welldoing; for if we faint not we shall reap in due season."

923   Senator Thomas Benton once replied to an opponent in a Senate debate, "I never quarrel, sir. But sometimes I fight, sir, and whenever I fight, sir, a funeral follows."

924   In 1863, when General Grant was fighting for control of the lower Mississippi, General Sherman wired to him, "Hold the Goddamn fort, I'm coming."

925   He who has a firm will molds the world to himself.—*Goethe*

926   The challenge is urgent; the task is difficult; the time is now.—*Victor Hugo*

927   There is no challenge of more grandeur than the meeting of a great crisis.—*Charles de Gaulle*

Responsibility

see CHALLENGE

928   Grover Cleveland, former President of the United States, was a man who became big but never considered himself too big to perform any task which might be required of him. He even once served as a hangman and hanged two criminals. This was while he was serving as sheriff of Erie County, New York. Rather than order this unpleasant task of hanging two men to be done by a subordinate, Cleveland did it himself.

929   We remember in Luke's Gospel the words of Jesus, "Unto whom much is given, much is required."

930   In *Under Western Eyes* by Joseph Conrad, Razumov, the middle-echelon bureaucrat, informs on his friend Haldin. Afterward, Razumov, disgusted with himself, goes to his superior, Councillor Mikulin, and says he wants to retire from the sordid affair.
    The councillor looks up.
    "To retire," he repeats.
    "Where to?" asks Councillor Mikulin.

931   It is often that I wake at night and begin to think about a serious problem and decide I must tell the Pope about it. Then I wake up completely and remember that I am the Pope. —*John XXIII*

932   The price of greatness is responsibility.—*Winston Churchill*

933   You cannot escape the responsibility of tomorrow by evading it today.—*Abraham Lincoln*

934   We cannot escape our dangers by recoiling from them. —*Winston Churchill*

935   Our responsibility: every opportunity, an obligation; every possession, a duty.—*John D. Rockefeller Jr.*

936   I feel the responsibility of the occasion. Responsibility is proportionate to opportunity.—*Woodrow Wilson*

937   To let oneself be bound by a duty from the moment you see it approaching is part of the integrity that alone justifies responsibility.—*Dag Hammarskjold*

Responsiveness

see LEADERSHIP

938   In the Old Testament, we remember how King Solomon, as a youth, was visited by an angel of the Lord. The angel asked the newly anointed king, "What gift do you most need to rule?"
    Solomon replied, "Give me an understanding heart."

939   The members of the House of Commons repeatedly tried to make King James I more accountable to them.
    Said King James, "I will govern according to the common weal, but not the common will."

940   Ole Bull, the nineteenth-century Norwegian violinist, was a man of singular simplicity of character. Once, as he was describing the grandeur of the hills and fjords of his native land, someone exclaimed, "Did you play to them, Ole?"
    "No," he replied, "I listened."

941   In classical mythology, the Greek god Antaeus drew his strength by keeping touch with the ground. He was impotent whenever he lost contact.

942   Over twenty-five centuries ago, Isaiah warned his people, "And let your soul delight not in fatness. Incline your ear."

Retirement

see FAREWELL, PUBLIC OFFICE, SERVICE

943   When Thomas Jefferson completed his two terms as President in 1809, he wrote: "Today I return to the people; my seat is with them."

944   When John Jay, one of the Founding Fathers, was asked how it was possible for him to occupy his mind after his retirement from public life, he said, "I have a long life to look back upon and an eternity to look forward to."

Revolution

see EXTREMISTS, RADICALS

945   Alexis de Tocqueville, referring to his French compatriots in revolutionary times, observed, "Halfway down the stairs, we threw ourselves out of the window to reach the ground more quickly."

946   In his novel *Under Western Eyes* Joseph Conrad has the narrator describe what must have been his own views about the course of revolution:

"A violent revolution falls into the hands of narrow-minded fanatics and of tyrannical hypocrites at first. Afterwards comes the turn of all the pretentious intellectual failures of the time. . . . The scrupulous and the just, the noble, humane, and devoted natures; the unselfish and the intelligent may begin a movement—but it passes away from them. They are not the leaders of a revolution. They are its victims. . . . Hopes grotesquely betrayed, ideals caricatured—that is the definition of revolutionary success."

947   They (the revolutionaries) forget the present for the future, the fate of humanity for the delusion of power, the misery of the slums for the mirage of the eternal city, ordinary justice for an empty promised land.—*Albert Camus*

948   Revolution is an idea which has formed its bayonets.—*Napoleon*

949   Insurrection of thought always precedes insurrection of arms.—*Wendell Phillips*

950   The time to stop a revolution is at the beginning, not the end.—*Adlai Stevenson*

951   Revolutions, as long and bitter experience reveals, are apt to take their color from the regime they overthrow.—*R. H. Tawney*

952   The free souls are in revolt. And you cannot meet a revolution with a referendum.—*Israel Zangwill*

953   The purity of a revolution can last a fortnight.—*Jean Cocteau*

954   When peaceful revolutions become impossible, violent revolutions become inevitable.—*John F. Kennedy*

955   Revolt and revolution both wind up at the same crossroads: the police or folly.—*Albert Camus*

956   Now the misfortune of revolutionists is that they are disinherited, and their folly is that they wish to be disinherited even more than they are. Hence, in the midst of their passionate and even heroic idealisms, there is commonly a strange poverty in their minds, many an ugly turn in their lives, and an ostentatious vileness in their manners. They wish to be the leaders of mankind, but they are wretched representatives of humanity.—*George Santayana*

Sacrifice

see MEMORIAL, SERVICE

957   The total sacrifice to a cause beyond his comprehension restored a richness to man.—*André Malraux*

958   Two basic ideas of modern man are in the Gospels—without them he is unthinkable—the idea of free personality and the idea of life as a sacrifice.—*Boris Pasternak*

959   At the grave of a hero who has done these things, we end not with sorrow at the inevitable loss, but with the contagion of his courage; and with a kind of desperate joy we go back to the fight.—*Oliver Wendell Holmes*

960   If man is not ready to risk his life, where is his dignity? —*André Malraux*

Scholar

see KNOWLEDGE, TEACHER, UNIVERSITY

961   The purpose of education is not happiness, it is not social integration, or political system. Its purpose is at once the discipline of the mind for its own sake; these ends are to be achieved through the mastery of fundamental subjects which cluster around language and numbers—the two chief instruments by which man knows himself and understands his relation to the world.—*Allen Tate*

962   It does not necessarily follow that a scholar in the humanities is also a humanist—but it should, for what does it avail a man to be the greatest expert on John Donne if he cannot hear the bell tolling?—*Milton Eisenhower*

963   While scholarship can clear the thickets, it can build little. —*Learned Hand*

Science

see TECHNOLOGICAL SOCIETY

964   C. P. Snow, British author and scientist, was appalled at the illiteracy of liberal arts people. He often asked them if they could describe the Second Law of Thermodynamics. Their response was negative.
    "Yet," said Snow, "that is about the scientific equivalent of 'Have you read a work of Shakespeare's?' "

965   To progress, even to survive, we must learn to apply the truths of God to the direction of science.—*Charles Lindbergh*

966   Science commits suicide when it adopts a creed.—*Thomas Huxley*

967   No amount of experimentation can ever prove me right; a single experiment can prove me wrong.—*Albert Einstein*

968   Men love to wonder, and that is the seed of science.— *Ralph Waldo Emerson*

969   As long as men are free to ask what they must—free to say what they think—free to think what they will—freedom can never be lost and science can never regress.—*Robert Oppenheimer*

970   Science is facts; just as houses are made of stones, so is science made of facts; but a pile of stones is not a house and a collection of facts is not necessarily science.—*Henri Poincaré*

971   Modern man worships at the temple of science, but science tells him only what is possible, not what is right.—*Milton Eisenhower*

972   Let both sides seek to invoke the wonders of science instead of its terrors. Together let us explore the stars, conquer the deserts, eradicate disease, tap the ocean depths and encourage the arts and commerce.—*John F. Kennedy*

973   Nature is neutral. Man has wrested from nature the power to make the world a desert or to make the deserts bloom. There is no evil in the atom; only in men's souls.—*Adlai Stevenson*

974   Man has mounted science and is now run away with.—*Henry Adams*

975   Science, like life, feeds on its own decay. New facts burst old rules; then newly divined conceptions bind old and new together into a reconciling law.—*William James*

976   Science is nothing but developed perception, integrated intent, common sense rounded out and minutely articulated.—*George Santayana*

Service

see CIVIC WORK, COMMITMENT, PUBLIC OFFICE, SACRIFICE

977   The poem, "True Religion," written by Tulsi Das, a sixteenth-century Hindu poet, was translated from the Sanskrit in 1930 by Mahatma Gandhi while he was imprisoned. One verse reads:

> Nothing is hard to him, who casting life aside
> Thinks only this
> How may I serve my fellowman?

978   James B. Conant of Harvard University had these words of counsel to the incoming president, Nathan Pusey:
"In this job you have two options: you can take the credit and get nothing done or you can get the job done by letting someone else get the credit."

979   In the twelfth century, the Bishop of Paris wrote to the Pope and asked to be given the assignment of a parish priest. He found the tasks much more arduous than those of bishop. The job of being out with the people administering to their needs was much harder than the paper-shuffling administrative work of the bishop. He wrote to the Pope, "It is far easier to be a saintly bishop than a Godly priest. Demote me and make me a bishop again."

980   The sole meaning of life is to serve humanity.—*Leo Tolstoy*

981   Open your eyes to the nobility of life and the sacred opportunities of service.—*Reform Jewish Prayer Book*

982   The two trusts that constitute the nobility of his calling: The service of truth and the service of freedom.—*Albert Camus*

983   You have not done enough, you have never done enough, so long as it is still possible that you have something to contribute. —*Dag Hammarskjold*

984   No one is useless in this world who lightens the burdens of another.—*Charles Dickens*

985   I am convinced that there is far more . . . of idealist will power than ever comes to the surface of the world . . . the idealism which becomes visible is small in proportion to what men and women bear locked in their hearts unreleased or scarcely released. —*Albert Schweitzer*

986   Every kind of service necessary to the public good becomes honorable by being necessary.—*Nathan Hale*

987   The real service is rendered by the man actually in the arena whose face is marred by dust and sweat and blood and serves valiantly.—*Theodore Roosevelt*

988   There is no higher religion than human service. To work for the common good is the greatest creed.—*Albert Schweitzer*

989   No man has ever risen to the real stature of spiritual manhood until he has found that it is finer to serve somebody else than it is to serve himself.—*Woodrow Wilson*

Soldier

see WAR

990   Once in a military ceremony Winston Churchill affixed a medal of bravery to a British soldier's tunic. Taking notice of the young man's apparent nervousness, Churchill said, "I am as awed of you just as you are apprehensive of me."

991   John F. Kennedy once told of a ditty found scratched on a sentry box in Gibraltar:

> God and the soldier all men adore
> In time of trouble and no more;
> For when war is over and all things righted
> God is neglected and the soldier slighted.

992   General Douglas MacArthur, honoring the American soldiers who fought so bravely in Bataan, said, "And all their yesterdays make possible our tomorrows."

993   Let the soldier yield to the civilian.—*Cicero*

994   If you believe the doctors nothing is wholesome; if you believe the theologians nothing is innocent; if you believe the soldiers nothing is safe.—*Lord Salisbury*

Solution

see CRISIS, PROBLEM, URGENCY

995   The antipoverty agency VISTA has this slogan which invites commitment: "If you're not part of the solution, you're part of the problem."

996   Always take hold of things by the smooth handle.—
Thomas Jefferson

997   Politics offers yesterday's answers to today's problems.—
Marshall McLuhan

998   To gain one's way is no escape from the responsibility for
an inferior solution.—*Winston Churchill*

999   I am interested in the next step, not the two hundredth.
—*Theodore Roosevelt*

1000   Some people seem to believe that for each problem there
is a solution readily available—a solution that can be promptly
achieved by passing a law and voting some money. I think of this
as the vending machine concept of social change. Put a coin in the
machine and out comes a piece of candy. If there is a social problem, pass a law and out comes a solution.—*John Gardner*

Specialization

see TECHNOLOGICAL SOCIETY

1001   For thousands of years, the civil-service exams in China
for positions in government include questions not about history,
economics, or geography, but questions about poetry.

1002   In 1950, Secretary of State Dean Acheson and the Chairman of the Joint Chiefs of Staff, General Omar Bradley, met in
a Washington restaurant to work out a common approach by State
Department and Pentagon officials to defense and foreign-policy
problems. It was agreed that neither group should respectively use
the phrase "from a purely military point of view" or "from a
purely political point of view" in discussing solutions. As leaders
with high responsibility they had to look at problems from all
sides, no matter what their special expertise was.

1003   We want a lot of engineers in the modern world, but we
do not want a world of engineers.—*Winston Churchill*

1004   Men are men before they are lawyers, physicians or manufacturers, and if you make them capable and sensible men they will

make themselves capable and sensible lawyers or physicians.— *John Stuart Mill*

Spending

see INFLATION, TAXATION

1005 Daniel Webster once reacted to a Jacksonian bank bill by slamming down his fist on his Senate desk and saying, "If this bill passes, charity will have to lend a mantle to wrap the pale corpse of a nation's credit."

1006 Some years ago at an embassy dinner in Washington, one envoy's wife wore a gown very décolleté, although nature had not endowed her with the necessary charms to wear such a garment.

The German minister gazed at her and then undiplomatically murmured, "She looks just like her country—an uncovered deficit."

1007 We remember Mr. Micawber's famous formula in Charles Dickens's *David Copperfield:* "Annual income twenty pounds, annual expenditure nineteen pounds six, result happiness."

1008 These federal billions are your money—your own money. Either they come out of your paycheck through higher taxes, or your pocket is picked by inflation.—*Dwight D. Eisenhower*

Statesmen

see GOVERNMENT, LEADERSHIP, POLITICS, PUBLIC OFFICE; also EXPEDIENCY

1009 In Shakespeare's *Henry V,* the Archbishop of Canterbury describes King Henry's statesmanlike skills:

> Turn him to any cause of policy,
> The Gordian knot of it he will unloose,
> Familiar as his garter. . . .

1010 Men are not great statesmen merely because they happen to have held great office.—*John Bright*

1011 A statesman is not an architect creating on a blank page, but a gardener cultivating forces of nature toward a decisive end. —*Sir Harold Nicolson*

1012 A constitutional statesman is in general a man of common opinions and uncommon abilities.—*Walter Bagehot*

1013 Great is the man who neither seeks nor shuns greatness, but who found glory only because glory lay in the plain path of duty.—*Thomas Macaulay*

1014 You can always get the truth from an American statesman after he has turned seventy or given up hope of the Presidency.—*Wendell Phillips*

1015 Statesmen are not called upon to settle the easy questions. These often settle themselves. It is when the balance quivers and the proportions are veiled in mist that the opportunity for world-saving decisions presents itself.—*Winston Churchill*

1016 A statesman cannot afford to be a moralist.—*Will Durant*

1017 A disposition to preserve and an ability to improve taken together would be my standards of a statesman.—*Edmund Burke*

1018 Statesmanship consists sometimes not so much in knowing what to do ultimately as in what to do now.—*Adlai Stevenson*

1019 The politician says, "I will give you what you want." The statesman says, "What you think you want is this, what it is possible for you to get is that. What you really want, therefore, is the following."—*Walter Lippmann*

1020 Statesmen must follow the clarified common thought or be broken.—*Woodrow Wilson*

1021 Great economic and social forces flow with a tidal sweep over communities that are only half conscious of them. Wise statesmen are those who foresee what time is bringing, and endeavor to shape institutions and to mold men's thought and purpose in accordance with the change that is silently surrounding them.—*Viscount Morley*

Taxation

see SPENDING

1022   In Dickens's *David Copperfield,* we remember Mr. Barkis telling David, "It was as true as taxes is, and nothing is truer than them."

1023   In his *Lives of the Caesars,* Suetonius wrote of Emperor Tiberius: "To provincial governors who wanted to raise taxes, he said, 'Good shepherds shear their sheep but do not skin them.' "

1024   Taxes are what we pay for civilized society.—*Oliver Wendell Holmes*

Teacher

see SCHOLAR, UNIVERSITY

1025   The core of the educational experience is the teacher/student relationship. It is best personified by the famous remark of President James Garfield that education meant sitting on a log with Mark Hopkins on one side and the student on the other:
  "Give one a log hut, with only a simple bench, Mark Hopkins on one end and I on the other, and you may have all the buildings, apparatus and libraries without him."

1026   The art of teaching is the art of assisting discovery.—*Mark Van Doren*

1027   A teacher who can arouse a feeling for one single good action, for one single good poem, accomplishes more than he who fills our memory with rows on rows of natural objects, classified with name and form.—*Goethe*

1028   A teacher affects eternity; no one can tell where his influence stops.—*Henry Adams*

1029   Teaching is not a lost art, but the regard for it is a lost tradition.—*Jacques Barzun*

Technological Society

see CIVILIZATION, MATERIALISM, SCIENCE, VALUES

1030   James Perkins, former president of Cornell, wrote to sociologist Margaret Mead his comments on youth:
"The most profound revolution . . . is the revolt against the social structures that require the individual to accept a role of specialization and subordination. . . . The individual is saying with increasing stridency that he will not accept this scenario either as a model of the good society or a model of the good life."

1031   In H. G. Wells's *The Time Machine,* the narrator realizes that the technological progress toward leisure and luxury has proved self-destructive, and he travels farther ahead into time, only to find all life on the planet gradually waning. He sees in the growing pile of civilization merely a "foolish heaping that must inevitably fall back upon and destroy its makers in the end."

1032   One cannot survey the American scene today without feelings of acute ambivalence. The performance of our economic system, the successes of our science and technology, the progress of improved education, the creative ferment among our young—all this quickens our hope. Yet we are dismayed by the failure and forces that dehumanize and defeat the finest dreams and plans of this generation. Nothing dishonors us more and does more to delimit the plans of general progress than the flaws that cause us to misunderstand the legacy of the past and misuse the opportunities of today.—*John Gardner*

1033   As we contemplate the world converted into a huge machine and managed by engineers, we gradually grow aware of its lack of meaning, of its emptiness of human value; the soul is stifled in this glorification of mechanical efficiency.—*Paul Elmer More*

1034   Unless the intellect of a nation keeps abreast of all material improvements, the society in which that occurs is no longer progressing.—*Winston Churchill*

1035 In their worship of the machine, many Americans have settled for something less than a full life, something that is hardly even a tenth of life, or a hundredth of a life. They have confused progress with mechanization.—*Lewis Mumford*

1036 People who trust themselves as machines are less and less able to feel toward themselves and other people.—*Rollo May*

1037 Technological wizardry is not an end in itself, it is desirable only if it makes for human welfare, and this is the test that any tool ought to be made to pass.—*Arnold Toynbee*

1038 There is, in truth, a terror in the world and the arts have heard it as they always do. Under the hum of the miraculous machines and the ceaseless publications of the brilliant physicists a silence waits and listens and is heard.—*Archibald MacLeish*

1039 The social problems raised by science must be faced and solved by the social sciences and the humanities.—*Harold Dodd*

1040 But I have seen the science I worshipped and the aircraft I loved destroying the civilization I expected them to serve.—*Charles Lindbergh*

1041 Without doubt machines will be able to determine the means and avenues to goals, but men will continue to set the goals themselves. For what machine can ever apply the considerations of compassion and justice which, as man's enlightenment spreads and his brotherhood awakens, will enter ever more often into the decisions that affect his future in the world.—*Lewis Strauss*

1042 We . . . repeatedly enlarge our instrumentalities without improving our purpose.—*Will Durant*

1043 The more humanity advances, the more it is degraded.—*Gustave Flaubert*

Time

see CHALLENGE, CRISIS, URGENCY

1044 "The earth is degenerating these days. Bribery and corruption abound. Children no longer mind parents. Every man wants to write a book and it is evident that the end of the world is approaching fast."

—Such was the prophecy inscribed on a tablet written in Assyria about 3000 B.C.

1045 "Many thinking people believe America has seen its best days."

—So wrote an influential Bostonian. He was the American patriot James Allen, and he wrote it in his diary July 26, 1775.

1046 In Matthew's Gospel, Jesus Christ is reported to have said, "You can predict the weather by looking at the sky. But why can't you see the signs of the times?"

1047 There is an ancient Chinese curse: "May you live in interesting times."

1048 Events are sometimes the best calendar.—*Benjamin Disraeli*

1049 Time has no divisions to mark its passing. There is never a thunderstorm to announce the beginning of a new month or year.—*Thomas Mann*

1050 It is indeed true that we live in tragic times. But too many people confuse tragedy with despair.—*Albert Camus*

1051 Mankind is now in one of its rare moods of shifting its outlook.—*Alfred North Whitehead*

1052 Prophecy is a fictitious and ungrateful business, but it hardly requires prophecy to foresee that men in future generations, if there are to be future generations, will look back on these few years as among the most terrible and splendid in the remake of the race.—*Archibald MacLeish*

1053 Ours is an age not of synthesis, but of analysis, not of constructive hopes but of awful destructive potentials, not of commitment, but of alienation.—*Kenneth Keniston*

1054 The clock indicates the moment—but what does eternity indicate?—*Walt Whitman*

Trial

see ORDEAL

1055 It is a rough road that leads to the heights of greatness. —*Seneca*

1056 But who can penetrate man's secret thought
The quality and temper of his soul
Till by high office put to frequent proof
And execution of the laws?

—*Sophocles*

1057 Wisdom and happiness consist in having recast natural energies in the furnace of experience.—*George Santayana*

Truth

see FACTS, KNOWLEDGE

1058 Edward R. Murrow, while director of the United States Information Agency, had this as a guiding philosophy:
To be persuasive, we must be believable,
To be believable, we must be credible,
To be credible, we must be truthful.

1059 In Henrik Ibsen's *An Enemy of the People,* Dr. Stockmann tells the editor, Hovstad, and a group of townspeople, why truth is not equivalent to the establishment:
"Yes, by Heaven, Mr. Hovstad! I intend to revolt against the lie that truth belongs exclusively to the majority. And what are these truths the majority worships? They're truths so old and worn—they're practically decrepit. And when a truth reaches that age you can hardly tell it from a lie!"

1060 The truth is so simple that it is regarded as pretentious banality.—*Dag Hammarskjold*

1061 Truth is a brief holiday between two long and dreary seasons during the first of which it is condemned as sophistry and during the second ignored as commonplace.—*Arthur Schopenhauer*

1062   Truth when not sought after rarely comes to life.—*Oliver Wendell Holmes*

1063   Truth has a way of shifting under pressure.—*Curtis Bok*

1064   For my part, whatever anguish of spirit it may cost, I am willing to know the whole truth, to know the worst and to provide for it.—*Patrick Henry*

1065   The strong are saying nothing until they see.—*Robert Frost*

1066   To stand inquiring right is not to stray,
To sleep or run is.—*John Donne*

1067   We lie loudest when we lie to ourselves.—*Eric Hoffer*

1068   Ridicule is the test of truth.—*William Hazlitt*

1069   The fact will one day flower into a truth.—*Henry David Thoreau*

1070   He who hides an evil, will perish from that evil.—*The Koran*

1071   Truth is a jewel; it can never be painted over, but it may be set to advantage in good light.—*George Santayana*

1072   Truth is a clumsy scullery maid who breaks the dishes as she washes them up.—*Karl Kraus*

1073   It is understandable when children are afraid of darkness but it is pitiable when adults are afraid of the light.—*Plato*

1074   "For example" is not proof.—*Yiddish proverb*

1075   It is not truth that makes man great, but man who makes truth great.—*Confucius*

Unity

see AMERICA

1076   In his inaugural address in 1801, Thomas Jefferson, publicly at least, buried the hatchet with the Federalist Party:

"Now, fellow citizens, that the contest of opinion through which we have just passed is over, let us unite with one heart and one mind. Let us restore social intercourse and banish political intolerance. We are all Republicans. We are all Federalists. Let us then with courage and confidence pursue our Federal and Republican principles; our attachment to the Union and representative government."

1077   When President Andrew Jackson was awarded an honorary degree from Harvard, a student seeking to embarrass the President called out from the audience, "Say something in Latin, Dr. Jackson." The well-bred sons of Harvard laughed and the voice cried again, "Say something in Latin, Dr. Jackson." The old man pivoted with the help of his cane, walked toward the audience, and said, *"E pluribus unum,* my friend! The *sine qua non."*

1078   John Winthrop was the first governor of the Massachusetts Colony. While crossing to America, he said to his fellow Puritans on the *Arbella,* "Now the only way to avoid this shipwreck and to provide for our posterity—we must be knit together as one man—we must entertain for each other brotherly affection . . . we must uphold a familiar commerce together . . . we must delight in each other, make others' conditions our own, rejoice together, mourn together, labor and suffer together."

University

see SCHOLAR, TEACHER

1079   When he was asked what it takes to make a university great, President Lowell of Harvard answered, "Three hundred years."

1080   Charles W. Eliot, famous president of Harvard University, was once told by a fellow educator: "Permit me to congratulate you on the miracles you have performed at the university. Since you became President, Harvard has become a storehouse of knowledge."

"That is true," laughed Eliot, "but I scarcely deserve the credit for that. It is simply that the freshmen bring so much knowledge in, and the seniors take so little out."

1081   When President Alexander Heard of Vanderbilt permitted the black militant Stokely Carmichael to speak at a university symposium in 1967, he was roundly criticized. Heard's reply:

"There is no use trying to make ideas safe for students, you have to make students safe for ideas."

1082   Following the riots at Columbia in 1968, the Law School published its Declaration of Conscience. One sentence read:

"Using muscles instead of minds has no place in the academic setting."

1083   Celibacy does not suit a university; it must mate itself with action.—*Alfred North Whitehead*

1084   Higher education is supposed to complete the foundation for a continuing process of learning that extends into professional and business life. Yet how can it do so if it lags behind the professional and business world in adapting to a new environment? If a business institution were to react so lethargically to the need for new concepts and procedures, its failure would be only a matter of time.—*Robert Sarnoff*

1085   A university does great things, but there is one thing it does not do; it does not intellectualize its neighborhood.—*John Henry Cardinal Newman*

1086   The university is the archive of the Western ideal, the keeper of the Western culture, the guardian of our heritage, the dwelling place of the free mind, the teacher of teachers.—*Adlai Stevenson*

1087   A liberal education is the education which gives a man a clear, conscious view of his own opinions and judgments, a truth in developing them, an eloquence in expressing them and a force in urging them.—*John Henry Cardinal Newman*

1088   A college education is not a quantitative body of memorized knowledge salted away in a card file. It is a taste for knowledge, a taste for philosophy, if you will, a capacity to explore, to question, to perceive relationships between fields of knowledge and experience.—*Whitney Griswold*

1089   Men must be born free; they cannot be born wise; and it is the duty of the university to make free men wise.—*Adlai Stevenson*

1090   My idea of education is to unsettle the minds of the young and inflame their intellects.—*Robert Maynard Hutchins*

1091   You may not carry a sword beneath a scholar's gown or lead flaming causes from a cloister.—*Learned Hand*

1092   A university . . . is a place which wins the admiration of the young by its celebrity—kindles the affection of the middle-aged by its beauty—and rivets the fidelity of the old by its association. —*John Henry Cardinal Newman*

Urgency

see CRISIS, PROBLEM, SOLUTION, TIME;
also APATHY

1093   While preparing for a battle, Napoleon told a messenger enroute to Paris: "Go, sir, and gallop and don't forget that the world was made in six days. You can ask me for anything except time."

1094   In Shakespeare's *Richard II,* Salisbury cries out, "O call back yesterday, bid time return."

1095   The moving finger writes; and having writ,
        Moves on; nor all your piety nor wit
        Shall lure it back to cancel half a line,
        Nor all your tears wash out a word of it.
                    —*Omar Khayyam*

1096   There is, however, a limit at which forbearance ceases to be a virtue.—*Edmund Burke*

Values

see MATERIALISM, PRINCIPLES, TECHNOLOGICAL SOCIETY

1097   Let us raise a standard to which the wise and honest can repair.—*George Washington*

Violence

see ANARCHY, EXTREMISTS, RADICALS, REVOLUTION;
also ORDER

1098   Fifteen hundred years ago the prophet Ezekiel said of Jerusalem: "This land is full of bloody crimes, and the city is full of violence."

1099   The symptom of ideology is impatience and its offspring is violence. Those who see the great turbulent issues of politics or law in simple terms of right and wrong are impatient with compromise or concession and even with reason.—*Henry Steele Commager*

1100   Violence, continually less restrained by the confines of a legality established over the course of many generations, strides brazenly and victoriously through the whole world, unconcerned with the fact that its sterility has already been manifested and proven many times in history. Nor is it merely brute force that triumphs but its trumpeted justification also: the whole world is being flooded with the crude conviction that force can do everything and righteousness and innocence nothing.—*Aleksandr I. Solzhenitsyn in his undelivered Nobel Prize lecture*

1101   Utopia is not a republic of fraternity to be taken by violence. Neither can it be taken by men who have no vision of better things for mankind.—*Norman Thomas*

1102   Some of you have knives, and I ask you to put them up. Some of you have arms, and I ask you to put them up. Get the weapon of nonviolence, the breastplate of righteousness and just keep marching.—*Martin Luther King, Jr.*

1103   Humanity is waiting for something other than blind imitation of the past. We must begin to turn mankind away from the long and desolate night of violence. May it not be that the new man the world needs is the nonviolent man?—*Martin Luther King, Jr.*

1104   In the tumult of civil discord the laws of society lose their force and their place is seldom supplied by those of humanity.—*Edward Gibbon*

1105   Destructiveness is the outcome of unlived lives.—*Erich Fromm*

1106   Violent disorder once set in motion may spawn tyranny, not freedom.—*Charles E. Wyzanski*

1107   Violence is counter-productive and produces changes of a sort you don't want. It is a very dangerous instrument and can destroy those who wield it.—*John Gardner*

1108   Do not shirk the imperative priority of the restoration of security in time of violence. Do not leave the tasks of dealing with violence to those who do not believe in the liberal and compassionate reforms of our society. For as violence mounts, the restoration of order becomes the first necessity of a civilization.—*Walter Lippmann*

1109   Violence has always achieved only destruction, not construction, the kindling of passions, not their pacification, the accumulation of hate and ruin, not the reconciliation of the contending parties.—*Pope John XXIII*

Vision

see BEGINNING, LEADERSHIP, RENEWAL

1110   As the White Queen said to Alice in *Through the Looking-Glass,* "It's a poor sort of memory that only works backward."

1111   Dreams are the touchstones of our characters.—*Henry David Thoreau*

1112   Moral education is impossible without the habitual vision of greatness.—*Alfred North Whitehead*

1113   If we all can persevere, if we can in every land and office look beyond our own shores and ambitions, then surely the age will dawn in which the strong are just and the weak secure and the peace preserved.—*John F. Kennedy*

1114   We must not lose our capacity to dream, to see, amid the realities of today, the possibilities of tomorrow. And then if we believe in our dreams—we must also wake up and work for them. —*Richard M. Nixon*

1115   Some men see things as they are and say *why?* I dream things that never were and say *why not?*—*George Bernard Shaw*

1116   Tell me, umbrella-mongers—when has an umbrella ever kept the rains and mist from entering a heart and shaping it with dreams?—*Muñoz Marín*

1117   No man that does not see visions will ever realize any high hope or undertake any high mission.—*Woodrow Wilson*

1118   In times when the passions are beginning to take charge of the conduct of human affairs, one should pay less attention to what men of experience and common sense are thinking than to what is preoccupying the imagination of dreamers.—*Alexis de Tocqueville*

1119   Dreams have as much influence as action.—*Lord Melbourne*

1120   History is certainly not bound to repeat itself and it actually fails to repeat itself more often than not. At the same time, history is also not bound not to repeat itself; and since it may repeat itself, our past experience is always worth bringing to bear when we are peering into the future.—*Arnold Toynbee*

Vocation

see EXCELLENCE

1121   "Madam, respect the burden," was Napoleon's advice to the housekeeper at St. Helena when she asked a group of people carrying loads to get out of the way for the emperor.

1122   A young Harvard student wrote home to his parents that he did not want to take up a professional career. He felt no call to enter the ministry, medicine or law. Discouraged but undaunted, Henry Wadsworth Longfellow closed his letter with this line: "Whatever I do, study ought to be engaged in with all my soul, for I will be eminent in something."

1123   Each honest calling, each walk of life, has its own elite, its own aristocracy based upon excellence of performance.—*James B. Conant*

1124   To do my duty in that state of life into which it shall please God to call me.—*Anglican Book of Common Prayer*

1125   I beseech ye to walk worthy of the vocation wherewith ye are called.—*Paul in his* LETTER TO THE EPHESIANS

1126   I hold every man a debtor to his profession.—*Francis Bacon*

1127   Every calling is great when greatly pursued.—*Oliver Wendell Holmes*

1128   We work not only to produce but to give value to time.—*Eugène Delacroix*

1129   It is well for a man to respect his own vocation whatever it is and to think himself bound to uphold it and to claim for it the respect it deserves.—*Charles Dickens*

1130   People do not inquire concerning a stranger, "What is he?" but "What can he do?"—*Benjamin Franklin*

1131   We are told that talent creates it own opportunities. But it sometimes seems that intense desire creates not only it own opportunities, but its own talents.—*Eric Hoffer*

1132   It is not society's fault that most men miss their vocation. —*George Santayana*

1133   Always take a job that is too big for you.—*Harry Emerson Fosdick*

War

see FOREIGN POLICY, SOLDIER;
also PEACE

1134 At the outbreak of World War I, the outgoing chancellor of Germany, Prince von Bülow, said to his successor, "How did it all happen?"

"Ah, if we only knew," was the reply.

1135 The Paris Art Show in 1969 exhibited a work of sculpture by Sibaja. It portrayed in red ice two prizefighters who bleed slowly into buckets under their boxing ring while a tape recorder plays screams from a crowd.

1136 War is only a cowardly escape from the problems of peace.—*Thomas Mann*

1137 The great danger of war seems to me not to lie in the deliberate actions of wicked men, but in the inability of harassed men to manage events that have run away with them.—*Henry A. Kissinger*

1138 War is a bad thing; but to submit to the dictation of other states is worse. . . . Freedom, if we hold fast to it, will alternately restore our losses, but submission will mean permanent loss of all that we value. To you who call yourselves ever of peace I say, you are not safe unless you have men of action at your side.—*Thucydides*

1139 War should be an instrument of national policy, but it should not be an instrument of a universal dream.—*Walter Lippmann*

1140 The next dreadful thing to a battle lost is a battle won.—*Duke of Wellington*

1141 There are no warlike peoples—just warlike leaders.—*Ralph Bunche*

1142 War would end if the dead could return.—*Stanley Baldwin*

1143   Every man, woman, and child lives under a nuclear sword of Damocles, hanging by the slenderest of threads capable of being cut at any moment by accident, miscalculation, or madness. The weapons of war must be abolished before they abolish us.—*John F. Kennedy*

1144   Killing one man is murder; killing thousands is a statistic. —*Robert F. Kennedy*

1145   It is always easy to begin a war, but very difficult to stop one, since its beginning and end are not under the control of one man.—*Sallust*

1146   A conscientious man would be cautious how he dealt in blood.—*Edmund Burke*

1147   "But what good came of it at last?"
                        Quoth Little Peterkin.
                        "Why, that I cannot tell," said he,
                        "But 'twas a famous victory."
                                    —*Robert Southey*

Welfare

see HUMANITY, POVERTY

1148   If you give a man a fish, he will have a single meal. If you teach him how to fish, he will eat all his life.—*Kuan-Tzu*

Women

1149   The last sentence of Goethe's *Faust* is a tribute to the power of women:
"Das Ewig-Weibliche zieht uns hinan." (The eternal feminine draws us on.)

1150   Dean Acheson once asked Justice Oliver Wendell Holmes what would be the subject of conversation if many of the great men of the ages were brought together in a single room.
    Said Holmes, "They would find a way to talk through a series of interpreters; and the talk would be about the one subject they would all have in common—women."

1151   Woman may be said to be inferior to man.—*Aristotle*

1152   Despite my thirty years of research into the feminine soul, I have not yet been able to answer . . . the great question that has never been answered: What does a woman want?—*Sigmund Freud*

1153   The only question left to be settled now is, are women persons?—*Susan B. Anthony*

1154   No amount of preaching, exhortation, sympathy, and benevolence will render the condition of working women what it should be so long as the kitchen and the needle are substantially their only resource.—*Horace Greeley*

1155   Women have served all these centuries as looking glasses possessing the . . . power of reflecting the figure of the man at twice its actual size.—*Virginia Woolf*

1156   Her best and safest club is the home.—*Grover Cleveland*

1157   They were Americans and they knew how to worship a woman.—*William Dean Howells*

1158   If I were asked . . . to what the singular prosperity and growing strength of that people ought mainly to be attributed, I should reply, to the superiority of their women.—*Alexis de Tocqueville*

1159   Think what cowards men would be if they had to bear children.—*George Bernard Shaw*

Youth

see IDEALISM;
also AGE

1160   When Horace Walpole taunted the thirty-two-year-old William Pitt because of his age, the young minister defended himself with this statement:
   "I will not attempt to determine whether youth can be imputed to any man as a reproach, but I will affirm that the wretch, who

after having seen the consequences of repeated errors, continues still to blunder, and whose age has only added obstinacy to stupidity, is surely the object of either abhorrence or contempt, and deserves not that his gray head should secure him from insult."

1161   In Plutarch's *Lives,* the historian cites the Roman statesman Cato on the generation gap:
"It was always risky for one generation to lecture the next."

1162   In July 1969, a law student, Meldon E. Levine, told the adult generation at his Harvard graduation:
"You have given us our visions and then asked us to curb them. You have offered us dreams and then urged us to abandon them. You have made us idealists and then told us to go slowly."

1163   As Biron says in Shakespeare's *Love's Labour's Lost,*
"Young blood doth not obey an old decree."

1164   At the death of Robert F. Kennedy, his brother, Senator Edward M. Kennedy, said this about the great deeds of young men:
"Some believe there is nothing one man or one woman can do against the enormous array of the world's ills. Yet many of the world's great movements of thought and action have flowed from the work of a single man. A young monk began the Protestant Reformation, a young general extended an empire from Macedonia to the borders of the earth and a young woman reclaimed the territory of France. It was a young Italian explorer who discovered the New World and the thirty-two-year-old Thomas Jefferson who proclaimed that all men are created equal."

1165   The very accomplishments of our generation—in technology, communications, affluence—have served to focus the attention of the young on what we have failed to accomplish.—
John D. Rockefeller 3rd

1166   America is the country of young men.—*Ralph Waldo Emerson*

1167   Youth is the trustee of posterity.—*Benjamin Disraeli*

1168   It is youth that has discovered love as a weapon.—*Peter Ustinov*

1169 When the young behave badly, it is because society has already behaved worse. We have the teen-agers like the politicians and the wars we deserve.—*J. B. Priestley*

1170 Youth is a continual intoxication; it is the fever of reason. —*La Rochefoucauld*

1171 If youth is a defect, it is one that we outgrow too soon. —*Robert Lowell*

1172 Come on now, all you young men, all over the world. . . . Twenty to twenty-five. These are the years. Don't be content with things as they are. "The earth is yours and the fullness thereof." Enter upon your inheritance, accept your responsibilities. . . . You will make all kinds of mistakes; but as long as you are generous and true, and also fierce, you cannot hurt the world or even seriously disturb her. She was made to be wooed and won by youth. —*Winston Churchill*

1173 Everybody's youth is a dream, a form of chemical madness.—*F. Scott Fitzgerald*

1174 The young have aspirations that never come to pass, the old have reminiscences of what never happened.—*H. H. Munro (Saki)*

1175 I shall go out with the chariots to counsel and command, for that is the privilege of the old; the young must fight in the ranks.—*Homer*

1176 Youth can measure in only one direction—from the things as they are forward to their ideal of what things ought to be. They cannot measure backward, to things as they used to be, because they have not lived long enough. And they cannot measure laterally to the condition of other societies because they have not yet the opportunity to know them well. . . . This is the core reason why the generation gap exists.—*Eric Sevareid*

1177 Let no youth have any anxiety about the upshot of his education whatever the line of it may be. If he keeps faithfully busy each hour of the working day, he may safely leave the final result to itself.—*Benjamin Cardozo*

1178   A social order is stable so long as it can offer scope to talent and youth. Youth itself is a talent—a perishable talent.—*Eric Hoffer*

1179   It's all that the young can do for the old, to shock them and keep them up-to-date.—*George Bernard Shaw*

1180   If we would guide by the light of reason, we must let our minds be bold.—*Louis Brandeis*

1181   Youth is wholly experimental.—*Robert Louis Stevenson*

1182   The use of the university is to make young gentlemen as unlike their fathers as possible.—*Woodrow Wilson*

Zeal

see IDEALISM;
also EXTREMISTS

1183   We remember Prince Talleyrand's cynical advice to diplomats: "Above all, no zeal."

1184   While Abraham Lincoln admired the efficiency of his Secretary of War, Edmund Stanton, he recommended handling his zeal this way:
"We ought to treat Stanton as they are sometimes obliged to treat a Methodist minister I know out west. He gets wrought up to so high a pitch of excitement in his prayers and exhortations that they put bricks in his pockets to keep him down. But, I guess we'll let him jump awhile first."

1185   Seek not the spirit, if it hide
    Inexorable to thy zeal.—*Ralph Waldo Emerson*

Soul-Shakers

1186   At the start of the Revolutionary War the Lutheran minister Peter Muhlenberg had some mixed feelings about whether he should fight. In January 1776 he resolved those feelings in a sermon to his Pennsylvania congregation.

Tearing off his black clerical garb to show a blue Continental Army uniform, he stepped down from the pulpit, saying, "There is a time to preach and a time to pray but there is also a time to fight and that time has come."

(And the time has come for us to stop asking and start acting . . .)

1187   We recall the story of the great French general, Marshal Louis Lyautey, who once asked his gardener in Algeria to plant a tree. The gardener objected saying, "Marshal, this tree is slow-growing and will not reach maturity for a hundred years." Lyautey replied, "In that case, there is no time to lose—plant it this afternoon."

(And we too have no time to lose . . .)

1188   When George Washington was positioned by the Hudson River in 1779, he called in a general known as "Mad Anthony" Wayne.

Said Wayne: "I'll storm hell, General Washington, if you will only plan the assault."

And Washington replied: "Perhaps, my dear General Wayne, we had better try Stony Point first."

(And so let us concentrate on this first step of getting . . .)

TO REMIND PEOPLE OF THE GREATNESS OF OUR HERITAGE

1189   In 1971 a woman presented a hand-sewn flag to President Nixon at the White House. When the President remarked how much effort must have gone into the making of the flag, she replied: "Yes, Mr. President, there are 78,000 stitches in that flag, but it was worthwhile because every one of those stitches stands for something that is right about America."

(And so let us begin to take the affirmative about America and . . .)

1190   More than 150 years ago, Andrew Jackson, then a militia general, issued a proclamation to rouse the citizens of Tennessee against the threat from abroad which resulted in the War of 1812.

"We are freeborn citizens," he said. "We are going to fight for the re-establishment of our national character."

(Today we Americans must fight for the re-establishment of our character . . .)

1191   There is a famous painting of the signing of the Declaration of Independence which hangs in the White House. It is unusual because for some reason the artist never finished it. Many of the figures in the background of the scene are only sketched in or left blank. That painting reminds us of a profound truth. The American Revolution is unfinished business, with important roles still open for each of us to play.

As President Nixon once said, "The message of that uncompleted painting is this: Any American can be a signer of the Declaration of Independence."

(And so let us pledge and commit ourselves . . .)

1192   In the 1870s the ambassador to the Court of St. James was the poet and writer James Russell Lowell. One day the French historian Guizot, who was also the ambassador to England, approached Lowell and asked, "Mr. Ambassador, how long will the American republic endure?"

Lowell replied, "As long as the ideals of its leaders reflect the ideals of the Founding Fathers."

(And let us hope that our forefathers' dedication to those ideals is matched by our dedication . . .)

TO BE USED TO INAUGURATE A PROGRAM
OR START A PROJECT

1193   At the close of the Revolutionary War in 1782, a Philadelphian remarked to his friend, Dr. Benjamin Rush, "It looks as if the battle for independence is finally over."

Rush replied, "Sir, you are mistaken. The Revolutionary War may be over, but the battle of independence has just begun."

(And so today we have begun what may be a continuing endeavor . . .)

1194   At the close of the Constitutional Convention, Benjamin Franklin rose and made an observation about the chair from which General Washington had been presiding.

On the chair was the design of a sun low on the horizon, and many of the delegates had wondered whether it was a rising or a setting sun.

"We know now," Franklin said. "It is a rising sun and the beginning of a great new day!"

(And today I see a rising sun and a new day . . .)

1195   On February 11, 1861, President-elect Abraham Lincoln made his departure from his home in Springfield, to begin the rail journey to Washington, where he was to be inaugurated. Standing on the rear platform of the railroad car, he bid his farewell, and closed with these words:

"Today I leave you. I go to assume a task more difficult than that which devolved upon General Washington. The great God which guided him must help me. Without that assistance I shall surely fail: with it, I cannot fail.

(And with your help and God's help we shall not fail . . .)

TO STIR AN AUDIENCE IN THE FIGHT AGAINST BIGOTRY

1196   Whenever the "better angels of our nature" are appealed to, we think of the man who first used that phrase—Abraham Lincoln. Let us also think of the epitaph he once said he wanted:

"When I die, I want it said of me that I always plucked a thistle and planted a flower where I thought a flower would grow."

(So let it be said of us that we plucked the thistles of prejudice and planted the flowers of brotherhood . . .)

1197   In 1682 William Penn met with the Delaware Indian chiefs at Shackamaxon (now Kensington in Philadelphia) to sign the treaty of friendship. He closed his address with these words:

"We are met on the broad pathway of good faith and good will, so that no advantage is to be taken on either side, but all to be openness and love."

(On such a highway of good faith and good will let us go forward . . .)

TO BE USED AS CLOSERS TO BUSINESS OR TRADE GROUPS

1198   As we face up to this task let us remember the advice given to us over a hundred years ago by Henry David Thoreau:

"It is truly enough said that a corporation has no conscience; but a corporation of conscientious men is corporation with a conscience."

(And let us with like conscience . . .)

1199   Just before the Revolutionary War Benjamin Franklin sent a message from London to Charles Thompson, the secretary of the Continental Congress:

"The suns of liberty are setting," he wrote: "we must light up the candles of enterprise and economy."

(So let us today begin to light some candles in behalf of . . .)

1200   Some sixty years ago in a Midwestern city, just after Theodore Roosevelt had given a speech, a member of the audience approached the speaker's platform and said, "Mr. President, I am just an ordinary businessman. What can I possibly do to help my country?"

And Theodore Roosevelt replied: "Do what you can with what you have got, where you are, but *do* it."

(And so let us vow today to do what we can to . . .)

TO MAKE THE AUDIENCE LOOK AT A GREAT PROBLEM
AS A CHALLENGE

1201   During the Civil War, when Admiral Du Pont told Admiral Farragut six reasons why he could not have taken his gunboats into Charleston harbor, Farragut replied: "But Admiral Du Pont, there was another reason that you have not mentioned."
"What is that?"
"You did not believe you could do it."
(And, gentlemen, because we believe we *can* do it we shall . . .)

1202   When in 325 B.C. the troops of Alexander the Great wanted to turn back from the march through India and return home to Macedonia, Alexander told them:
"Difficulties are only steps to a goal: the courageous man calls them challenges."
(Let us mount the first step of challenge by . . .)

TO USE AS CLOSERS TO CHURCH OR RELIGIOUS GROUPS

1203   More than a century ago a wise French visitor came to America. He patiently sought the greatness and genius of America in our fields and in our forests, in our mines and in our commerce, in our Congress and in our Constitution, and he found them not. But when he sought further, Count Alexis de Tocqueville said:
"Not until I went into the churches of America and heard her pulpits flame with righteousness did I understand the secret of her genius and power. America is great because America is good— and if America ever ceases to be good—America will cease to be great."
(And in that call to righteousness let us strive . . .)

1204   In A.D. 67 the Apostle Paul found himself jailed by Nero's edict in a Roman prison. The great missionary, now close to death, gave a Christian visitor, Onesiphorus, a message to deliver to his assistant who was almost a son to him, Timothy. It was the final message from the pen whose writings changed history.
The note declared: "I have fought a good fight; I have finished the course; I have kept the faith."

(Let us like Paul make the church into such an active force that we can say to our children we have fought the good fight and have kept the faith . . .)

1205   We remember the story of the prophet Amos. The Lord called out to him, "Amos, what do you see?" Amos replied, "I see a wall." Then the Lord said, "What do you see beside the wall?" And Amos replied, "I see a plumb line." "Behold," said the Lord, "I am setting a plumb line to find out how straight the people of Israel stand."

(And so today let us show how straight and tall we stand in our faith by . . .)

TO URGE THE AUDIENCE TO GUARD
THEIR CONSTITUTIONAL RIGHTS

1206   When Abraham Lincoln made his way from Springfield to Washington to be inaugurated as the sixteenth President, he often made speeches from the back of the train to citizens at various cities. At one stop, he told them that the future of democracy depended on the commitment of each of them:

"I appeal to you to constantly bear in mind that not with the politicians, not with the President, not with the office-seekers, but with you is the question: 'Shall the liberties of this country be preserved to the latest generations?' "

(And so the question I put to you is shall the right to . . .)

1207   At the time of the enactment of the Bill of Rights, Thomas Jefferson in Monticello wrote to his friend Dr. Benjamin Rush in Philadelphia: "I have sworn upon the altar of God eternal hostility against every form of tyranny over the mind of man."

(And let us swear our hostility to any attempt . . .)

TO URGE THE AUDIENCE TO TAKE A STAND
AND ACCEPT RESPONSIBILITY

1208   We remember King Belshazzar's Feast, when the fingers of a man's hand wrote on the wall of the palace these words: *Mene, mene, tekel upharsim.* (You have been counted. You have been weighed. You have been found wanting.)

(Today each of us is going to have to stand up and be counted as we . . .)

1209   There is a story told in Syria of an old wise man in Damascus who could answer any riddle of life. One day, a young boy decided to journey to Damascus to play a trick on the old man.

"I will capture a bird, hold it cupped in my hands, and then ask whether it is dead or alive. If he says 'dead,' I'll let it fly away, if he says 'alive,' I will crush it before opening my hands."

With the cupped bird in his hands, the boy went to the old man and asked, "Is the bird I have in my hands dead or alive?"

The old man replied: "Lad, the answer is in your hands."

(And so in your hands is the question . . .)

TO REMIND PEOPLE OF THEIR OBLIGATION
TO MAKE THEIR CITY A BETTER PLACE

1210   Perhaps the birthplace of what we call civic spirit was Athens. It was the obligation of each Athenian when he became twenty-one to take this oath in the public square before his family and neighbors:

"We will strive unceasingly to quicken the public sense of duty so that we will make this city greater, better, and more beautiful than it was when we took this oath."

(And so we have the chance to make our city better for our children by . . .)

1211   The first piece of land General Eisenhower ever owned was the farm he bought in Gettysburg after World War II. When he was asked by the recording clerk in the Gettysburg County Courthouse at the time of settlement why he wanted to have that property, he replied, "When I die, I want to leave a piece of ground better than I found it."

(And so let us endeavor to make our community . . .)

1212   When Governor John Winthrop in 1630 called together his Puritan passengers on the flagship *Arbella* to meet the task of building a new colony, he told them: "We must always consider that we shall be as a city upon a hill—the eyes of all people upon us."

(And the eyes of all people will be on our community as we try . . .)

TO URGE AN AUDIENCE TO DO WHAT THEY KNOW IS RIGHT

1213 When Abraham Lincoln in 1860 came to Cooper Union as an aspiring Presidential candidate, the audience expected him to temporize on the slavery issue. But Lincoln did not.

Instead, he flatly opposed the extension of slavery, saying:

"Let us have faith that right makes might, and in that faith let us to the end dare to do our duty as we understand it."

(And in that faith let us today dare to do . . .)

1214 Today we have the choice between what seems the popular course and what we know to be the right course. In that respect we recall the words of General Douglas MacArthur on his eighty-fourth birthday. As he emerged from the Waldorf-Astoria hotel, he was asked by newsmen what he saw to be the central issue facing man.

The general replied: "The world is in constant conspiracy against the brave. It's the age-old struggle: the roar of the crowd on one side and the voice of your conscience on the other."

(Gentlemen, we know what the voice of conscience tells us today . . .)

1215 When Abraham Lincoln was being censured for his unwavering policy in defense of the Union, he gave this answer to his critics:

"I am not bound to win, but I am bound to be true. I am not bound to succeed, but I am bound to live up to what light I have. I must stand with anybody that stands right: stand with him while he is right and part from him when he goes wrong."

(Gentlemen, we may not be bound to win this struggle but we are bound to stand up and . . .)

1216 When Martin Luther, at the fateful Diet of Worms on April 18, 1521, challenged the Assembly of Prelates, he said,

"Here I stand—I cannot do otherwise. God help me! Amen."

(And today we cannot do otherwise, as we stand for . . .)

1217   Let us hope that someday we may feel like John Morton, the Continental Congress delegate whose deadlock-breaking vote in the Pennsylvania caucus was a major factor in the adoption of the Declaration of Independence.

As he lay dying, broken by the rejection of his own constituents who disapproved of his action, he said, "Tell them that they will live to see that hour when they shall acknowledge that my act in that hour to have been the most glorious service that I ever rendered to my country."

(Today we can render a service to our country by declaring ourselves . . .)

TO BE USED TO CLOSE SPEECHES TO DOCTORS
OR MEDICAL ASSOCIATIONS

1218   The man who established the first free medical clinic in the United States was also the only doctor to sign the Declaration of Independence. Shortly before he died in 1814 he lectured his students: "If a tombstone be afforded after my death to rescue my humble name for a few years from oblivion, I ask no further addition to it than that 'I was an advocate for principles in medicine.' "

(In that spirit let us go on to do more . . .)

TO STRESS THE IMPORTANCE OF EDUCATION

1219   In the sixteenth century Queen Elizabeth noted the presence of one of her favorite courtiers, Sir Walter Mildmay, who had been missing from court for some time.

"Sir Walter," she said, "where have you been?"

Mildmay, who had been away establishing Emanuel College at Cambridge, replied, "Madam, I have been away planting an acorn. And when it becomes an oak, God only knoweth what it will amount to."

(And so let us plant the seed . . .)

1220   The man who probably gave the most for the cause of American education was Horace Mann. Mann gave up a promising legal career to build up the Massachusetts public school system. He never regretted that decision. Only days before he died, in 1859, he gave a final speech at Antioch College saying:

"Be ashamed to die until you have won some victory for humanity."

(And today we can win victory for humanity by . . .)

1221   In the Spanish Civil War Franco's army forced the closing of the University of Salamanca. As one of the generals arrested the Spanish philosopher Miguel de Unamuno, he shouted the Falangist slogan, "Long live the glory of war."

And Unamuno replied, "Long live the glory of knowledge."

(And for the glory and betterment of education let us . . .)

TO CLOSE A SPEECH ABOUT POLLUTION OR WASTE

1222   The last speech Adlai Stevenson ever gave was to the United Nations in July 1965, a few days before his death.

"We travel together," he said, "passengers on a little spaceship, dependent on its vulnerable reserves of air and soil: all committed for our safety to its security and peace: preserved from annihilation only by the care, the work, and I will say the life we give our fragile craft."

(Let us with love preserve those vulnerable reserves . . .)

1223   In the early nineteenth century, when the U.S. government was pressuring Indian tribes to leave the Midwestern territories, one official approached Tecumseh, the great warrior chief, who replied, "Sell the country! Why not sell the air, the clouds, the great sea?"

(And, gentlemen, we cannot sell . . .)

TO URGE THE AUDIENCE TO PLACE THEIR TRUST IN GOD

1224   On D-Day, 1944, as the Allied forces began their momentous invasion of Normandy, King George VI addressed by radio the embarking British armies. He closed his address with this invocation:

"We ask not that God may do our will but rather that we may do His will."

(And in the faith that we are carrying out His will let us . . .)

1225 During the Constitutional Convention in 1787 Benjamin Franklin rose to offer a motion to begin each session with prayer.

"I have lived, sir, a long time," he said, "and the longer I live the more convincing proofs I see of this truth, that God governs in the affairs of men. And if a sparrow cannot fall to the ground without His notice, is it probable that an empire can rise without His aid?"

(And so with the invocation of His aid let us endeavor . . .)

1226 But let us be mindful of the words of Saint Augustine: "I shall work as if everything depended on me. I shall pray as if everything depended on God."

1227 In the midst of the Civil War a delegation of Methodist clergy called on President Lincoln at the White House. They assured Lincoln that the Union cause would prevail because God was on their side.

But Lincoln wisely replied: "Gentlemen, it is not a question of whether God is on our side. It is a question of whether we are on His side."

(With that faith let us hope and pray to be on His side . . .)

TO REMIND THE AUDIENCE OF THEIR DUTY
TO PREPARE NOW FOR THE FUTURE OF
THEIR CHILDREN AND POSTERITY

1228 More than two hundred years ago a twelve-year-old shop boy in the West Indies wrote in his diary his ambition: "I mean to prepare the way for futurity."

(That boy was Alexander Hamilton and like him we can help prepare the way in building a better society . . .)

1229 In Philadelphia the highest landmark is the statue of William Penn on the top of the City Hall. On the base of this memorial to Penn is the biblical inscription: Lo—I go to prepare a place before thee.

(Today we must prepare a place for our children and our children's children . . .)

1230   When the Roman Empire began to disintegrate in the fourth century B.C., Symmachus, the great Roman senator, petitioned Emperor Valentinian II to preserve the old Roman customs and traditions. He closed his appeal with these words: "Grant, we beseech you, that what we received as children, we may as elders transmit to our posterity."

(And so in the hope that we may transmit to our children . . .)

1231   It is good to recall these last words President Eisenhower spoke to his wife, Mamie, just before he died:

"I have always loved my wife, I've always loved my children, I've always loved my grandchildren, and I've always loved my country."

(If we love our children and our country, we should . . .)

TO REMIND THE AUDIENCE OF THEIR DUTY
TO HELP THOSE IN NEED

1232   During the Civil War President Abraham Lincoln received hundreds of appeals for pardons from soldiers who were sentenced to death by military tribunal. Each appeal was, invariably, supported by letters from influential people. One day, a single sheet came before him—an appeal from a soldier without any supporting documents.

"What," exclaimed the President, "has this man no friends?"

"No, sir, not one," said the adjutant.

"Then," said Lincoln, signing the pardon, "I will be his friend."

(And so let each of us be a friend by . . .)

1233   Shortly after his election, Pope John XXIII set out one morning for the first of a series of visits to Italian prisons.

Asked by one of his aides to explain his reasoning for such a tour he replied, "Why, they cannot come to see me, so I must go to see them."

(And so let us today reach out to those . . .)

TO MAKE PEOPLE REALIZE THAT EACH OF US
HAS SOMETHING TO CONTRIBUTE

1234   Not long ago I was told about a minister who on a Saturday afternoon was trying to write his Sunday sermon but was bothered by his six-year-old son. Exasperated, he cut up into little bits a newspaper page showing a picture of the world. He told the boy to go up to his room and put the pieces together. In a short time he returned.

The father asked, "How did you do it so quickly?"

"It was easy, Daddy. On the back of the page of the map was the face of a man. You see, Daddy, when the man is right, the world is right."

(And so each of us can help make the world right by contributing in our own life . . .)

1235   When in the 1840's William Lloyd Garrison began his lonely crusade against slavery, he started his own newspaper and printed on the masthead the courageous words:

> I am in earnest
> I shall not excuse
> I shall not equivocate
> I shall not retreat a single inch
> And I shall be heard

(And so let each of us be heard . . .)

TO URGE PEOPLE TO BECOME PART OF THE ENDEAVOR
TO MAKE A BETTER SOCIETY

1236   In 1628 Captain John Smith, the pioneer of Virginia, wrote in his diary: "I would rather be a settler in America than Good Queen Bess on the throne of England. Here one can spread his wings and soar like eagles. These are the times for men to live."

(And these are also great times for men to live. We, too, can be part of a great adventure . . .)

1237   In 1965 one of the world's noblest public servants, Dag Hammarskjold, died in a plane crash on a UN peace mission in Africa. Among the notes in his diary he left behind were these words:

"In our time the road to holiness leads into and through the field of action."

(And let us get on the field of action by . . .)

1238　In 1910 Woodrow Wilson, president of Princeton, was drafted as the nominee for governor of New Jersey. In his acceptance speech he issued this call for action:

"Someday when we are dead, men will come and point at the distant upland with a great shout of joy and triumph and thank God that there were men who undertook to lead in the struggle. What difference does it make if we ourselves do not reach the uplands? We have given our lives to the enterprise. The world is made happier and humankind better because we have lived."

(And so let us commit ourselves to this enterprise . . .)

1239　There is a plaque in the lobby of the Hotel de Crillon in Paris. The reason for the plaque goes back to 1589 when King Henry IV of France won a bloody victory at Arques, while his erstwhile friend and supporter Crillon stayed away. The message that Henry IV supposedly sent to Crillon is now emblazoned on the hotel wall:

"Hang yourself, brave Crillon. We have fought at Arques, and you were not there."

(And let it not be said of us that we were not there when the fight to . . .)

TO CLOSE A COMMEMORATIVE ADDRESS OR EULOGY

1240　My thoughts at this time go back hundreds of centuries ago to some verse carved on the rocks of Thermopylae where a few Greeks in 480 B.C. valiantly withstood thousands of Persians. The words read:

Go passer-by and to Sparta tell
That we in faithful service fell.

(And so let us with memory of his faithful service . . .)

1241　When Theodore Roosevelt learned of the death of his son, Quentin, in World War I, he wrote these lines:

"Only those are fit to live who do not fear to die and none are fit to die who have shrunk from the joy of life. Both life and death are parts of the same great adventure worthily carried through by the man who puts his personal safety first. But all of us who gave service, and stand ready for service, are torch bearers. We run with the torches until we fall . . ."

(And so let us run with the torches to . . .)

1242   Perhaps the most appropriate words when death comes are those songwriter Alan J. Lerner wrote at the death of his friend Maurice Chevalier: "I envy the angels."

(And so too I look at heaven as a brighter place . . .)

1243   The story of the Unknown Soldier buried in Arlington National Cemetery started with an Army sergeant named Younger who was viewing the closed coffins of unidentified World War I dead. He was to choose one by placing a white rose on one of them. As he told it later, he was walking by one of the caskets, when a voice seemed to say, "This is a pal of yours."

(Today, we honor some who were friends of all of us . . .)

TO URGE THE AUDIENCE TO CARRY A MESSAGE
OR SPREAD THE WORD

1244   In 1780 in Hartford, Connecticut, the skies at noon turned one day from blue to gray and by mid-afternoon the city had darkened over so densely that, in that religious age, men fell on their knees and begged a final blessing before the end came. The Connecticut House of Representatives was in session and many of the members clamored for immediate adjournment. The Speaker of the House, one Colonel Davenport, came to his feet and then silenced the din with these words:

"The Day of Judgment is either approaching or it is not. If it is not, there is no cause for adjournment. If it is, I choose to be found doing my duty. I move, therefore, that candles be brought to enlighten this hall of democracy."

(Let each of us in this difficult time bring the candles to help enlighten our society . . .)

1245   When a Canadian dignitary at the Vatican asked Pope John XXIII to explain his objective in calling the Ecumenical Council, the Pope walked over to the window, opened it and said, "What do we intend to do? We intend to let in a little fresh air."

(Let us today open some windows by . . .)

TO BE USED IN SPEECHES TO BLACK AUDIENCES

1246   To avoid a problem is not to answer it. Escape may be the easy way, but not the right way. As the black writer James Baldwin has written:
"Not everything that is faced can be changed but nothing can be changed until it is faced."
(We can begin facing things and changing things by . . .)

1247   And I want to leave you with a line from a poem by the black poet Langston Hughes: "What happens to a dream deferred? Does it dry up? Or does it explode?"
(Let us help bring a dream to pass by . . .)

TO LOOK AT THE FUTURE AS AN OPPORTUNITY

1248   In the fifteenth century Spain considered itself the westernmost point of civilization and emblazoned on its coat of arms *ne plus ultra,* or, "nothing more beyond." But when Columbus returned from his voyage in 1493, Queen Isabella decided to have the motto repainted.
The new phrasing eliminated the *ne* and read *plus ultra,* or, "more beyond."
(Today, "more beyond" awaits us as . . .)

1249   When Franklin D. Roosevelt died in Warm Springs, Georgia, in 1945, he was posing for a portrait and thinking over a speech he was to have made.
A fragment of that unfinished speech exists and reads: "The only limit to our realization of tomorrow is our doubts of today."
(And there is no limit to the opportunities before us . . .)

TO CLOSE A SPEECH ON WORLD PROBLEMS

1250   Let us be mindful of what Pope John XXIII said to Norman Cousins shortly before his death:
"World peace is mankind's greatest need. I am old but I will do what I can in the time I have."

(And so let us do what we can at this time to make . . .)

1251 Dr. Robert Oppenheimer, who supervised the creation of the first atomic bomb, was once called before a congressional committee. During the questioning, a Congressman asked: "Doctor, is there any defense against the nuclear weapon?"

"Certainly," Dr. Oppenheimer replied, "it is peace."

(We will be closer to such peace if today we . . .)

1252 If there is any American whose life and service symbolized the search for peace, it was Woodrow Wilson. His was the vision of a world made secure by the rule of law under a League of Nations.

When he was asked in 1920 why he was giving so much of himself to this cause, he said: "My clients are the children: my clients are the next generation."

(It is for our children, for peace in our children's world that we must . . .)

1253 The late war correspondent Marguerite Higgins used to tell a story that happened in the midst of the Greek Civil War in 1947. In a small village there was a gathering to say farewell to a fellow townsman who was emigrating to South America. And when he asked what he should send back, an old villager replied, "Send a ton of tranquillity."

(And let us help send some peace and tranquillity across the world by . . .)

TO ADVANCE A SOLUTION OR OFFER A NEW PROPOSAL

1254 In 1777 Benjamin Franklin was asked by a Frenchman what the prospects were for success for the American struggle for independence. Franklin replied, in a phrase that became a slogan and then a patriotic hymn:

"*Ça ira, ça tiendra!*" (It will grow, it will catch on.)

(And we know that this idea that we have talked about today is also one that will catch on . . .)

1255 In 1825, General Lafayette made a return visit to the country whose independence he helped secure. Anxious to see how this experiment in self-government was making out, he toured the cities and towns of the emerging republic.

Afterward, he wrote to a colleague these words which evinced his faith in the American democracy:

"They are solving the magnificent problem of liberty."

(So in that spirit let us solve the problem of . . .)

TO STRESS TO THE AUDIENCE THE HEADWAY
OR SUCCESS ALREADY MADE

1256   In 1820 Simón Bolívar, in answer to a question of how long the struggle to free all the rest of the countries in upper South America from Spanish rule would take, wrote: "We are now seeing the light and it is not our desire to be thrust back in the darkness."

(And now as we are beginning to see the light we look confidently . . .)

TO STRESS THE IMPORTANCE OF LAW AND JUSTICE
IN A FREE SOCIETY

1257   Many centuries ago in the marketplace of Athens the philosopher Thucydides was asked by a fellow citizen, "When will justice come to Athens?"

And Thucydides replied: "Justice will not come to Athens until those who are not injured are as indignant as those who are injured."

(And justice will not come to our society until we wake up . . .)

TO GET THE AUDIENCE BEHIND A CERTAIN
MEASURE FOR REFORM

1258   During some congressional investigations of land sales before World War I, Boston lawyer Louis Brandeis appeared before the committee as a representative of a group of citizens alarmed at the waste. When he took the witness stand, a Congressman challenged his right to be present.

"Who, sir," he asked, "do you represent? Who is the client retaining you?"

"I, sir," replied the future Supreme Court Justice, "represent the people. The public is my client."

(And so let us as advocates for the people . . .)

1259   Émile Zola was the man who redressed one of the great injustices in history, the Dreyfus case. When he died, his fellow author Anatole France knelt at his coffin and said: "He was a moment in the conscience of history."

(Today we too can become a moment in the conscience of history . . .)

TO REMIND THE AUDIENCE OF THE IMPORTANCE
OF SCIENTIFIC PURSUITS

1260   When Commander Neil Armstrong was invited to address the Joint Session of Congress after his moon voyage, he told them, "Man must understand his universe in order to understand his destiny."

(And this project today will better enable us to understand . . .)

1261   A few years ago two British scientists made a major biological breakthrough in their discovery of the "double-helix cell." When they rushed out of their Cambridge University laboratory, friends asked them what the commotion was about.

They replied: "We have discovered the secret of life."

(And similarly we can make great strides in discovering the secrets . . .)

1262   When the famous German mathematician Karl Jacobi was asked why he decided to spend his life in the pursuit of such abstractions, he replied, "For the honor of the human spirit."

(And in that spirit let us endeavor to continue . . .)

TO STRESS THE REWARDS OF COMMUNITY
AND PUBLIC SERVICE

1263   The story has been told that the young William Penn was once asked by an acquaintance to take him to a Quaker meeting in London. The future founder of Pennsylvania did so. When the friend had sat through an hour of silence, he puzzledly asked Penn, "When does the service begin?"

And Penn replied: "The service begins when the meeting ends."
(Today as this meeting ends, let us begin to serve . . .)

1264   Some years ago Alice Freeman Palmer, then president of
Wellesley College, was told by her husband that she should retire
and devote herself to writing. She rejected his advice saying:

"It is people that count—you put yourself in people, they touch
other people; these, others still, and so you go on working forever."

(And you too can go on working forever by carrying on these
endeavors . . .)

TO EXPRESS THE IDEAL OF ATHLETIC EXCELLENCE
OR GREATNESS

1265   When Manager Red Rolfe of the Detroit Tigers was asked
why he hired the old veteran Yankee Charlie Keller to join the
team, he replied: "I didn't hire Charlie Keller because he was a
Yankee or because we're friends or because I wanted to do him a
favor. I hired him because I wanted to give the ball club a touch of
class."

(And a touch of class is what . . .)

1266   Whitney Young once told of his meeting with Jackie Robinson's son, who said that he received from his father a legacy that
meant a lot more than money or rank.

Said the boy: "He has left me a name that means courage and
guts."

(And so the man we honor tonight has forged a name that
means . . .)

1267   When Captain James Cook, the eighteenth-century English
explorer of the Pacific, was asked why he felt the call to explore,
he said, "I had not the ambition only to go farther than any other
man, but as far as man can go."

(And in establishing this record . . .)

TO PLEA FOR AUDIENCE SUPPORT AND HELP

1268   During the early days of World War II, when England
stood alone against Germany, President Roosevelt sent to Winston

Churchill a Longfellow poem written out in his own hand. To a hushed House of Commons, Churchill asked for permission to read the verse aloud:

> Sail on, O Ship of State!
> Sail on, O Union, strong and great!
> Humanity with all its fears,
> With all its hopes of future years,
> Is hanging breathless on thy fate!

When he had finished, Churchill looked up and said, "What is the answer that I shall give to this great American leader? Here it is: Give us the tools and we will finish the job."

(And so I say, give us your support and we will finish the job of . . .)

1269   In a little town in southern Italy there had been a statue of Christ that had been shattered by the enemy in World War II. The village priest led the townspeople in a search through the rubble for the pieces. Eventually, most of the statue—head, body, legs— was pieced together, but as hard as they searched, they could not find the hands. Finally, in despair, they asked the priest what to do with the reconstructed statue of Christ without the hands.

"Children," replied the padre, "you are his hands."

(And so let us lend our hands to finish . . .)

1270   When Charles de Gaulle assumed the presidency of France in 1958, he spoke by radio to the French people, closing his address with these words:

"It was dark yesterday. But this evening there is light—French-women, Frenchmen, help me."

(And with your help, we are going to succeed in . . .)

TO BE USED TO CLOSE SPEECHES TO LABOR
OR UNION GROUPS

1271   Many years ago, the great labor leader Samuel Gompers was asked the question: "What does labor want?"

"What does labor want?" he replied. "We want more school-houses, fewer jails; more books and fewer arsenals; more learning and less vice; more leisure and less greed; more justice and less revenge; in fact, more of the opportunities to cultivate our better natures, to make manhood more noble, womanhood more beautiful, and childhood more happy and bright."

(And let us work for those better opportunities by . . .)

1272   During the Middle Ages, three stonemasons were asked what they were doing as they were working on their jobs.

One looked down and said, "I am shaping stone."

And the second looked up and said, "I am making a wall."

But the third proudly proclaimed, "I am building a cathedral."

(And so today let each of us with like vision see our role in building . . .)

1273   When Eugene Debs was jailed in Chicago during the Pullman strike, he received this telegram: "Stand by your principles regardless of consequences. Your Father and Mother."

(And standing by those principles of unionism we shall . . .)

TO REMIND THE AUDIENCE OF THE NEED
TO STAND TOGETHER

1274   In the spring of 1945, as the Allied armies were about to cross the Rhine in Germany, General Dwight Eisenhower, in the twilight of a foggy evening, ran into a G.I. restlessly pacing by the riverbank.

"What's the matter, soldier?" he asked.

The young man, not recognizing the Supreme Allied Commander said, "I guess I am a little nervous."

"Well, so am I," said General Eisenhower. "Let us both walk together by the river and perhaps we'll both draw strength from each other."

(And with the strength that comes from unity let us . . .)

1275   We all know how the Declaration of Independence begins, but do we know how it ends? Do we know what the last sentence was before the Founding Fathers signed their names?

These are the last words: "And for the support of this Declaration, with a firm reliance on the protection of Divine Providence, we mutually pledge to each other our lives, our fortunes, and our sacred honor."

(And gentlemen, like our Founding Fathers who committed themselves unitedly, let us pledge to . . .)

TO STRESS THE URGENCY FOR IMMEDIATE ACTION

1276   When we look at the present crisis we might think of what Justice Oliver Wendell Holmes told Franklin Roosevelt in 1933. Roosevelt had just been inaugurated, and one of his first acts was to make a call of respect upon the ninety-year-old Justice Holmes.

"Mr. Justice," said Roosevelt in those Depression days, "you have lived in one half of the history of our nation. What advice for an incoming President can you give to me at this time?"

Replied Holmes: "Mr. President, you are in a warlike crisis. When in war, my advice is to marshal your battalions and fight."

(So as we face this similar crisis today, let us marshal our resources and act now . . .)

1277   Shortly after his installation in 1958, Pope John XXIII gave word that he wanted to have a Vatican Council. A curial elder, advising Pope John of the tremendous difficulties in organizing such a conference, said, "We can't possibly have a Vatican Council by 1963."

John answered, "Then we will have one by 1962."

They did.

(Today the necessity of being ready faces us and we must look to the problem of getting . . .)

TO CLOSE A SPEECH TO AN AUDIENCE OF WOMEN

1278   Perhaps the first voice raised in America on behalf of women was Abigail Adams, who wrote to her husband, John, at the time of the adoption of the Declaration of Independence:

"I long to hear that you have declared an independence—and by the way in this new code of law I desire you would remember the ladies. . . ."

(And let us remember the ladies by . . .)

TO INSPIRE AND MOTIVATE YOUTH AND STUDENTS

1279 Almost a century and a half ago a young man tried to make his maiden speech in the British House of Commons but was hooted and laughed at.

But the young Benjamin Disraeli who was to become prime minister faced the mocking benches and said: "I will sit down but the time will come when you will hear of me."

(And so too are we going to be hearing from you and your generation . . .)

1280 Near the close of the nineteenth century a young man sent his manuscript of poetry to the man he considered to be the greatest man in American letters. Ralph Waldo Emerson read the work called *Leaves of Grass,* and wrote back to Walt Whitman:

"I greet you at the beginning of a great career."

(And so I greet you at the beginning of what may be your great careers . . .)

1281 Close to fifty years ago a class valedictorian at UCLA gave a memorable speech. His name was Ralph Bunche, and the future UN statesman said:

"Humanity's problem today is how to be saved from itself. If we are to develop our personalities to their fullest, we must add a fourth dimension to this ordinary self—that we may expand up and out from our narrow, immediate world. This fourth dimension —call it bigness, soulfulness, spirituality, imagination, altruism, vision, or what you will—is that quality which gives full meaning and true reality to others."

(And Ralph Bunche brought meaning to his words. So can you bring meaning to your life and career ahead . . .)

1282 When the former Czech leader Alexander Dubček was asked by protesting Prague students what was the best guarantee of a free and progressive government, he replied, "You are that guarantee. You, the youth of our country are that guarantee."

(And *you* are the guarantee that . . .)

Subject Index

A NOTE ON USING THE INDEXES

Throughout the book, the anecdotes are numbered. In the indexes the numbers shown refer to these numbered anecdotes except in the cases of unnumbered material. Then a page number is given, and "p." in **bold-face** type precedes the number.

235

Name Index

239

Crillon, Louis de, 1239
Crockett, Davy, 51

Dante, 93, **p. 35**
Danton, Georges Jacques, 83
Darrow, Clarence, **p. 23**
Das, Tulsi, 977
Davenport, Col., 1244, **pp. 42, 43**
De Gaulle, Charles, 62, 322, 470,
　596, 610, 718, 927, 1270
De Mille, Cecil B., **p. 35**
De Pew, Chauncey, **p. 28**
Debs, Eugene, 1273
Delacroix, Eugène, 1128
Demosthenes, 316, **pp. 8, 40**
Descartes, René, 405
Dewey, Thomas, 217
Dickens, Charles, 332, 753, 984,
　1007, 1022, 1129, **pp. 23, 35**
Dickinson, John, 294
Diderot, Denis, 780
Disraeli, Benjamin, 16, 35, 36, 129,
　158, 266, 500, 555, 757, 882,
　1048, 1167, 1279, **pp. 16, 35,
　36, 53, 56**
Dodd, Harold, 370, 1039
Donne, John, 353, 914, 1066
Dostoevski, Fëdor, 141, 247, 493,
　499, 851
Dreyfus, Alfred, 1259
Drucker, Peter, 269
Du Pont, Samuel, 1201
Dubček, Alexander, 1282
Dulles, John Foster, 357, 594
Dunne, Finley Peter, 551
Durant, Will, 172, 427, 681, 745,
　834, 1016, 1042

Eckhardt, Wolf von, 97
Edison, Thomas, 3
Ehrenburg, Ilya, 119
Einstein, Albert, 231, 699, 901, 967
Eisenhower, Dwight D., 63, 74, 155,
　346, 383, 404, 425, 527, 649,
　695, 705, 732, 1008, 1211,
　1231, 1274, **pp. 7, 37**
Eisenhower, Mamie, 1231
Eisenhower, Milton, 962, 971
Eliot, Charles W., 1080
Eliot, T. S., 265, 379

Elizabeth I, Queen, 422, 1219, 1236
Elizabeth, Queen Mother, 420
Emerson, Ralph Waldo, 76, 183,
　195, 225, 242, 261, 283, 481,
　506, 525, 544, 645, 763, 792,
　968, 1166, 1185, 1280, **p. 3**
Erskine, Thomas, 582
Ervin, Sam, **p. 37**
Ethelred, King, 240, **p. 39**
Euripides, 921
Eve, *see* Adam and Eve
Ezekiel (prophet), 1098

Falkland, Lord, 187
Faraday, Michael, 129
Farragut, David, 1201
Faulkner, William, 462
Ferdinand, King, **p. 23**
Fitzgerald, F. Scott, 865, 1173
Flaubert, Gustave, 1043
Forster, E. M., 906
Fosdick, Harry Emerson, 1133
Fox, George, 899
France, Anatole, 1259
Franco, Francisco, 1221
Frankfurter, Felix, 190, 746
Franklin, Benjamin, 160, 879, 885,
　1130, 1194, 1199, 1225, 1254,
　pp. 8, 35, 42, 45, 47–48
Freud, Sigmund, 1152
Fromm, Erich, 258, 263, 720, 1105
Frost, David, 461, **pp. 25–26**
Frost, Robert, 1065, **p. 35**
Fuller, Buckminster, 472

Gambetta, Léon, 384, 802, **p. 38**
Gandhi, Mahatma, 977
Gardner, John, 88, 151, 153, 180,
　205, 310, 313, 465, 475, 505,
　520, 603, 614, 837, 888, 897,
　1000, 1032, 1107
Garfield, James A., 288, 1025
Garrison, William Lloyd, 1235
Gauguin, Paul, 122
George VI, King, 1224
George, Henry, 548
Gibbon, Edward, 299, 589, 784,
　831, 1104
Gide, André, 123

73 74 75 76 77 10 9 8 7 6 5 4 3 2 1